healthy comfort foods

Gluten-free, diabetic-friendly, and keto recipes

BOBBI PIKE
WITH GEOFF PIKE

© 2024 Bobbi Pike

Library and Archives Canada Cataloguing in Publication
Title: Healthy comfort foods : gluten-free, diabetic-friendly, and keto recipes / Bobbi Pike ; with Geoff Pike.
Names: Pike, Bobbi, author. | Pike, Geoff, (Database manager), contributor.
Description: Includes index.
Identifiers: Canadiana 20230582230 | ISBN 9781989417881 (softcover)
Subjects: LCSH: Comfort food. | LCSH: Gluten-free diet—Recipes. | LCSH: Sugar-free diet—Recipes. | LCSH: Ketogenic diet. | LCSH: Low-carbohydrate diet—Recipes. | LCGFT: Cookbooks.
Classification: LCC RM219 .P55 2024 | DDC 615.8/548—dc23

Published by Boulder Books
Portugal Cove-St. Philip's, Newfoundland and Labrador
www.boulderbooks.ca

Design and layout: Tanya Montini
Editor: Stephanie Porter
Copy editor: Iona Bulgin

Printed in China

Excerpts from this publication may be reproduced under licence from Access Copyright, or with the express written permission of Boulder Books Ltd., or as permitted by law. All rights are otherwise reserved and no part of this publication may be reproduced, stored in a retrieval system, or transmitted in any form or by any means, electronic, mechanical, photocopying, scanning, recording, or otherwise, except as specifically authorized.

We acknowledge the financial support of the Government of Newfoundland and Labrador through the Department of Tourism, Culture, Arts and Recreation.

Dedication

I treasure my grandmother's cookbooks. She did not write them; they merely touched her hands as she worked the dough and stirred the soup. She took the time to pen her own notes in the margins to preserve her tweaks and personal touches. Those notes in faded ink mean more to me than all the fancy, authored cookbooks that grace my shelves.

I often wonder if she knew how much her jotted notes would mean one day. Did she write them only for herself or did she envision her words being passed on to future generations?

You, my son, should never have such a question. These recipes are all for you. One day in the not-so-distant future you will look back over these recipes and remember me. You will think of my meatballs, covered in sauce, tucked into my bacon-filled freezer. You will remember me trying to convince you to try the blackened salmon even though you weren't a salmon fan. You will reminisce about my trip to your Alberta home and the kitchen takeover where we made so many meals together. You will remember me in the kitchen and being silly in the aisles at the shops …

You will one day make my Addie's Cream Pie recipe with your own kids and tell them that Nanny wrote this recipe just for you.

Alex, you changed my life for the better. I've always told you that Momma love comes from a very special place in the heart and that it is like no other love. The love that I feel for you is truly the purest there is, so fierce and strong it takes my breath away at times. No matter what else I achieve in life, you are my masterpiece. You will always be my greatest recipe.

To Addie, with love.

Table of Contents

Preamble 7

Appetizers and Snacks 13
Baked Garlic Breadsticks 14
Chicken Nuggets 16
Cranberry Meatballs 18
Devilled Egg Unwich 23
Dill-Lightful Wings with Dill Aioli 24
Hickory Sticks 26
Lamb Kofta with Pomegranate Jam 29
Pan-Seared Scallops with Champagne Reduction 30
Pork Belly with Five Spice and Sticky Phoenix Sauce 32
Warm Bacon Dip 35

Breakfast and Brunch 37
Avo BLT Chaffle 38
Baked Cinnamon French Toast 41
Bell Pepper Egg Rings 43
Blueberry Pancakes 44
Fish Cakes Eggs Benny 46
Greek Omelette 50
Ham, Mushroom, and Tomato Hash
    with Sunny-Side-Up Eggs 53
Mushroom Pie 54
Quiche Lorraine 56
Salsa Egg Skillet 58

Soups and Stews 61
  Celeriac, Leek, and Bacon Soup 63
  Chicken and Ginger Noodle Bowl 64
  Cream of Chicken Soup 68
  Fennel Soup 73
  Italian Wedding Soup 74
  Jalapeño Popper Soup 77
  Portuguese Fish Stew 79
  Roasted Green Tomato Soup 80
  Stinging Nettle Soup 83
  Taco Soup 85
  White Asparagus (Spargel) Soup 86

Veggie Dishes and Sides 91
  Avocado and Tomato Salad 93
  Best Faux-Tato Salad 95
  Braised Baby Bok Choy 96
  Eggplant Lasagna with Béchamel 98
  Faux Mac and Cheese 103
  Faux Tater Tots 104
  Fennel Slaw 106
  Irish Colcannon 108
  Oven Roasted Veg 111
  Ratatouille—Imam Bayildi 113
  Ravioli with Brown Butter Sauce 116
  Roasted Carrots with Carrot Top Chimichurri 120
  Skeddi Ohs 122
  Sunday Roast Confit Faux-Tatoes 125
  Veggie Curry—Nine Gem Korma 127
  Whole Roasted Cauliflower 128

Fish Entrées 131
  Blackened Salmon 132
  Cod in Tarragon Butter 134
  Crispy Caesar Salmon 137
  Fish Stick Tacos 139
  Lemon and Dill Baked Cod 142
  Piccata Style Trout with Capers 144
  Salmon en Papillote 146
  Soused Shrimp 148
  Turmeric-Crusted Cod with Tomato Jam 151

Meat Entrées 153
  Braised Beef Ribs and Daikon 154
  Cheesy Beef Bake / Taco Pie 156
  Chicken à la King 159
  Chicken Lombardy 161
  Creamy Carbonara Primavera with Bacon 163
  Egg Roll in a Bowl 164
  Grilled Spatchcock Chicken with Maple Garlic
    and Cinco de Mayo BBQ Sauces 169
  Honey-ish Balsamic Pork Chops 173
  Lemon Chicken 174
  Masala-Spiced Pork Chops 177
  Mongolian Beef 179
  OMJ Half-Baked Chicken 180
  Pork Chops with Mushroom Ragout 182
  Pork Chops with Irish Whiskey Sauce 184
  Red Pepper Meatloaf 187
  Roasted-Garlic-and-Parm-Coated Pork 189
  Seared Duck Breast with Cherry Gastrique 190
  Shepherd's Pie 192
  Slow-Roasted Maple Pork Loin with
    Sun-Dried Tomatoes and Mushrooms 194
  Stuffed Polpette al Sugo—Meatballs
    in Red Sauce 197

Desserts ... 199

- Addie's (Billy Miner) Cream Pie ... 200
- Banana Cream Pie ... 202
- Blissfully Cran-Bars ... 205
- Blizzards ... 207
- Blondies ... 209
- Blueberry Cream Cake ... 210
- Boston Cream Poke Cake ... 212
- Chocolate Chip Cookie Skillet ... 217
- Chocolate Faux Guinness Cake
    with Irish Whiskey Frosting ... 218
- Cinnamon Coffee Cake Loaf ... 220
- Cranberry Cheesecake with
    White Chocolate Mousse ... 222
- Crustless Salted Caramel Cheesecake ... 225
- Dark Chocolate Tart with Raspberry Coulis ... 227
- Double Chocolate Peanut Butter Bars ... 230
- Faux Apple Cake Two Ways ... 232
- French Vanilla Ice Cream ... 237
- Ginger Crème Brûlée ... 240
- Jamaican Rum Cake ... 242
- Lilac Love Cake ... 244
- Lime Chiffon Cake with Praline Crumb ... 249
- Lisa and Brett's Nanaimo Cheesecake ... 253
- Mixed Berry Crumble Squares ... 254
- Peony and Pistachio Cake ... 256
- Roly Poly ... 259
- Shortbread Cookies ... 260
- Sour Cream Glazed Donuts ... 262
- Strawberry and Cream Mini Muffins ... 265
- Strawberry Shortcake Deconstructed ... 267
- Walnut Ginger Carrot Cake ... 269

Extras and Sauces ... 271

- Bacon Mayonnaise ... 272
- Baker's Magic (Pan) Release ... 273
- Blackberry Grill Sauce ... 273
- Cheese Ball ... 274
- Cocktail Sauce ... 274
- Donair Meat and Sweet Sauce ... 276
- Eggnog ... 278
- Figgy(less) Pudding ... 279
- Honey Mustard Glaze ... 281
- Jakey Buns (Tea Biscuits) ... 283
- Maple Syrup Substitute ... 283
- Marshmallow ... 284
- Mustard Vinaigrette Dressing ... 285
- Peanut Butter Granola ... 286
- Protein Pizza Crust—Margherita Pizza ... 289
- Soured Dough Bread ... 290
- Spinach Dip ... 292
- Tartar Sauce ... 293
- Teriyaki Sauce ... 293
- White Chocolate ... 295

Pantry Items ... 296
Index ... 301
Acknowledgements ... 303
About the Authors ... 304

Preamble

The kitchen has always been a place of wonder for me. A place where you can magically create experiments that you get to eat. A pinch of this, a flick of that, and voila. Dinner time.

When you take the romance out of the kitchen, it's all about chemistry, isn't it? If I add this to the experiment, what will happen?

Sometimes you have to be a baby goat and just play! For me, it stems from having no fear of failure in the kitchen. If it flops, it's only a few ingredients. No big deal. It doesn't mean that I am a failure; it just means that the project I am working on isn't finished yet.

You cannot be afraid to experiment and grow. I'm sure you've heard that baking is an exact science and you should never stray from a recipe. That's hogwash. How can we grow if we don't test our boundaries? In the pursuit of being a little better than we were the day before, shouldn't we challenge "the same"?

As a recipe creator, one part of my job is to try to fool up a recipe and anticipate issues. So if a reader has difficulties, I will be able to help figure out what went wrong. Why did the sauce split? Why didn't this rise? Why did this cake fall? I've messed up many recipes, only to turn them back into something edible again, and you can too.

I can tell you that 99 per cent of all the flops were fixed and eaten. They were not all perfect; there were many fixes and repeats. It's usually still edible even if it's not perfect. At one time, they all were works in progress.

I rarely used recipes and when I did, I would instinctively make the recipes my own. Many of my creations came from Nan's cookbooks and her notes, but for the most part, I only used the concept of the dish and, instead, followed my own instincts. When the recipe called for a teaspoon, something internal would automatically increase or decrease that amount. While I was in the pantry, I would spy another food item that went with what I was making.

I intuitively knew what went with what. The first time I made an alfredo sauce, I threw the meal together (without a recipe). The meal was lovely, but something was missing. Nutmeg! I had no idea why I thought the recipe needed nutmeg; I had never looked at an alfredo recipe, nor watched any tutorials on the subject. Geoff took curiosity into his own hands and googled and found it hilarious that each alfredo recipe he looked at called for nutmeg.

> I met Bobbi and Geoff many years ago at a culinary event that we all attended. I was doing my chef thing and Bobbi was a presenter of her beautiful art. Over the years our families became friends, and we met again and again at events and otherwise. In time, I invited Bobbi and Geoff to help me out at events; they did the same for others in the industry.
>
> Being so creative—and such a food lover—it only made sense that Bobbi would move her focus to culinary interests. Her efforts really took off when she and Geoff began their health journey with the keto lifestyle.
>
> Bobbi once said to me that she and Geoff felt rather intimated about stepping into a chef's role at events, especially in the presence of other, longer-established chefs. I told them that what they do is chef-worthy and that the public will decide if they should continue. The public has spoken resoundingly! Given their huge personal and professional success, it is obvious that Bobbi and Geoff filled an important niche with their recipes and cookbooks.
>
> They have been a great addition to the chef world and the culinary community in this province and beyond.
>
> Bobbi and Geoff are chefs because they are not afraid to try, they are willing to make mistakes, and they always try to surpass their last plate. I am honoured to have been able to help them out even in a small way. Chef on!

—Roary MacPherson, Executive Chef, Cannery Kitchen and Social

When we started our health journey, it was all about weight loss. We knew something had to change—so we did. We could not yet see the big picture. We thought that we would lose a few pounds and then go back to what we were used to. Were we ever wrong. Sure, we could have stopped quite easily, but the bigger question is—why would we?

What started as a temporary diet had turned into a way of life. For us, success came when we realized that we could eat the same type of foods, just tweaked a little. If not better than the original recipe, then just as good. If you could eat a more delicious, healthier version of the foods you're eating now, wouldn't you?

I've always been food-addicted. A handful of chips or popcorn instead of eating just one. Scrabbling up the leftovers in the pan while I'm supposed to be washing up. My tail end sticking out of the refrigerator at 3 a.m. because I was wanting more.

No more. I have discovered that if you're eating the right foods, and eliminate the fillers, you can eat to your heart's content. Food becomes comfort food without guilt.

"My first introduction to Bobbi Pike and Geoff was through word of mouth: 'Have you met Bobbi Pike? You must meet her and Geoff!' While in Newfoundland for my first (but not last!) trip, I heard much ado about East Coast Culinary for almost two days before setting eyes on them. That is how much they are respected and loved.

I finally met Bobbi and Geoff and the only thing sweeter and better then meeting them was tasting their food at a local culinary festival.

Having studied gluten-free and diabetic-friendly recipes, I know that the same problems always tend to surface: expensive and overcomplicated.

Not so with Bobbi's cookbook. Her food is simple to make, ingredients are easy to find, and above all else, delicious.

I am so happy to have met the faces behind East Coast Culinary; I have made a friendship that will delight my tummy for a lifetime."

—Elisabetta Mottiar, Chef Professor, Niagara College of Culinary Arts

Bobbi Pike with chefs Laura Bonin, Elisabetta Mottiar, and Craig Youdale of Niagara College of Culinary Arts.

In *Healthy Comfort Foods*, I have compiled my favourite food experiments. I've tried to jam-pack as many of the whys and hows into the book to help the home cook join me on this journey.

Before we move on, let's establish some housekeeping points. My recommendation is to not blindly follow these or any recipes. Any successful dish is only 80 per cent recipe; the rest is user interpretation, kitchen conditions, and culinary intuition. A kitchen is a place where you must think on your feet for success. Here are some general tips to keep in mind as you use the recipes in this book.

Always default to an oven temperature of 350°F unless otherwise specified.

Whipping cream will always be 35 per cent (or what's comparable in your area).

Choose a high-quality olive oil. Olive oil is graded by acidity. Extra virgin olive oil has a free fatty acid of 0.8 per cent or lower; virgin is 0.8 to 2 per cent. Every olive oil starts with an acidity level of zero, and then acidity rises if the olives are harvested too late. Extra virgin has grassy notes; for a more neutral tasting oil, opt for virgin or light olive oil.

Cocoa should always be measured in heaping spoonfuls. If you're overzealous and add too much cocoa, add a teaspoon of white or apple cider vinegar. Cocoa can add bitterness and the vinegar will neutralize this.

Any deep-fried foods can be baked; just add a thin layer of oil to the baking sheet before placing it in the oven.

If switching from a conventional to a forced air oven or an air fryer, decrease the oven temperature by 25°F.

Butter will always be salted. Use room temperature (and not melted) ingredients whenever indicated, especially butter. Heating butter will separate the milk solids and water from the butter fat, and once they separate, they will not go back together.

Vinegar will be your choice of either apple cider or white unless otherwise specified in the recipe.

Salt is either a Himalayan pink or sea salt and never table salt (which often contains sugar).

Sweetener is usually powdered. Sweeteners can be grainy and don't perform the same way sugar does. Buy granulated form, and use a compact blender to powderize them before use.

It's important to know your sweeteners. Some sweeteners, particularly erythritol, may recrystallize easily. For this reason, we recommend using a blend of sweeteners. Our recommendation is erythritol-monk fruit blend, but even with this combination the ratios of the blend, or even the amount of sweetener used, can be too much for a recipe and cause recrystallizing. If you find that a recipe is not sweet enough, try adding a little liquid stevia instead of more of the same sweetener that you've already used.

In traditional cooking, sugar is often omitted as a dry ingredient and instead reserved to be creamed into the butter. This mechanically leavens or whips air into the mix and also helps to emulsify or receive the liquids and other batter ingredients. The main sweetener we use, erythritol, is not hygroscopic, that is, it does not absorb liquid from its surroundings or bond to liquids the same way that sugar does. For this reason, in our recipes the sweetener is specified to be added with the other dry ingredients.

If you're looking for sweetener insight, refer to the article "The good, the bad and the ugly" on our website (all links are provided at the end of the book). The definition for healthy pasta and bread will depend on whether you're gluten-free, low carb, diabetic, or keto.

If you're gluten-free and are okay with using sugar, you can swap out the sweetener in these recipes with an equal measure of sugar.

White (carb) replacements such as konjac pasta or cauliflower rice, while lower in carb value than traditional foods, are still a little carb heavy. We recommend consuming no more than 1/4 cup of these foods as a serving.

"Having had the pleasure to visit Newfoundland and Labrador the past few years, I can say the province is a true unexplored Canadian treasure. Fantastic scenery, with salt-of-the-earth people.

I had the pleasure of meeting a talented artist named Bobbi Pike. We shared many meals together, none more memorable than the feast with Chef Mark McCrowe's trout cooked over a campfire—Bobbi's take on that recipe is in this book. Hallelujah, Amen, it was sensational, real food for real folk. It was so good we ate it with our fingers.

I have followed and experienced some of Bobbi's culinary creatives and she has become a dual professional with paint brush in one hand and sharp kitchen knife in the other.

Excited to have a preview of *Healthy Comfort Foods*, last night I cooked her recipe for roasted carrots with carrot top chimichurri. All the recipes in this book are approachable for cooks of all levels, with step-by-step, totally uncomplicated instructions. I smiled as I viewed each of the recipes and realized they're all healthy, and they all inspire a feeling of enjoyment—no rabbit food here!

Bobbi Pike rocks the Rock with real food."

—Chef John Higgins, Haggisracer

Many who use konjac or shirataki noodles complain about the difference in bite. As these don't have the doughy mouthfeel of a traditional noodle, our recommendation is to cut them so you can enjoy the pasta with fewer bites.

If using xanthan gum, be careful of adding it all at once unless it is being added with the dry ingredients. This ingredient is very easy to overuse and can also clump quickly if not in constant motion while being added. If adding it to liquids, try mixing it first with 1/8 teaspoon oil, or use an immersion blender while adding a little at a time.

Use these recipes as guidelines, general starting places for your own kitchen masterpieces. Your family's tastes may require more (or less) sweetness or spiciness. By the time you read these recipes, I will have already tweaked them again for my own personal tastes—I do each time I cook them, and I suggest you do the same. Use the white spaces on the pages to record your own tweaks, just as my grandmother did years ago.

If you have any questions about unfamiliar ingredients, refer to our pantry list at the end of the book.

Let's get cooking.

Appetizers and Snacks

Before You Go ...

Baked Garlic Breadsticks
Chicken Nuggets
Cranberry Meatballs
Devilled Egg Unwich
Dill-Lightful Wings with Dill Aioli
Hickory Sticks
Lamb Kofta with Pomegranate Jam
Pan-Seared Scallops with
    Champagne Reduction
Pork Belly with Five Spice
    and Sticky Phoenix Sauce
Warm Bacon Dip

Appetizers and starters can be hard to navigate. They're found in social settings and are generally not healthy, as they're often high in carbs and full of additives and preservatives.

These nibbles will get you every time. One nibble turns into one more, and then it's just as well to have another, isn't it? You blink and six months of straying from your eating plan have passed and you're right back to square one, and even more frustrated with yourself.

These are the times when it pays to be prepared. If you know the host and can ask ahead of time if it's okay to bring a dish to share, do it. Most hosts will be open to guests bringing a dish, especially if it's a crowd-pleaser. No need to get into dietary restrictions or preferences in any way. It's just food! If it's an event where you have no control, fortify yourself before you go.

Let's get smart about food, leave the food guilt behind, and learn to do this (life) by making a few small changes and tweaks to healthify the food we're consuming.

Before you go out on the town, make yourself one of these recipes.

Baked Garlic Breadsticks

▶ **EXTRA: ROASTED GARLIC BUTTER**

1 cup almond flour
1 tbsp egg white powder
1-2 tsp garlic powder, or to taste
1 tsp onion powder
1/2 tsp dried thyme
1/2 tsp dried parsley
1/2 tsp cream of tartar
1/4 tsp baking soda
1/4 tsp xanthan gum
8 oz grated mozzarella cheese
2 large eggs

Sometimes you just need a breadstick to smear across a plate. In this recipe, traditional dough is tweaked by removing most of the carbs, allowing you to enjoy a breadstick or two without blowing your daily carb allowance.

Spread out the dough and cut into soldiers (long narrow strips, reminiscent of those we used to dip into egg yolks) or, alternatively, form the dough into cylindrical-shaped loaves.

Try them with Roasted Garlic Butter.

1. Line a baking sheet with parchment paper. Set aside.
2. Combine all the dry ingredients in a large mixing bowl. Add the cheese and toss to coat. Make a well in the centre of the coated cheese and add the egg. Mix thoroughly. Use 1/4 to 1/2 cup extra flour if the dough is too sticky.
3. Refrigerate the dough for at least 15 minutes. Cover with plastic wrap if refrigerated for more than 30 minutes.
4. Form the dough by hand into a thick layer on the prepared baking sheet. Use the curve of your hand to create an outside edge as you form the crust. Cover the formed dough with another sheet of parchment paper and bake at 350°F for 10 minutes.
5. Remove the baking sheet from the oven and, using the parchment paper as handles, flip the dough. Alternatively, cover the baking sheet with another equal-sized baking sheet and turn everything upside down, forcing the dough to fall onto the new pan.
6. Remove the top layer of parchment and bake for another 10 minutes.
7. Let cool slightly and cut with a knife or pizza cutter.

▶ **ROASTED GARLIC BUTTER**

For extra decadence, spread a little roasted garlic butter on the breadsticks. Coat the individual garlic cloves with oil and roast at 275°F until they are soft and creamy. Continue with the following:

1/2 cup butter, at room temperature
1 oz grated Parmesan cheese
2 garlic cloves, roasted until soft, then mashed
1 tbsp fresh parsley, or 1 tsp dried parsley
1/4 tsp pepper

Combine all the ingredients. Use a food processor to achieve extra creaminess. Refrigerate the garlic butter in an airtight container.

Chicken Nuggets
▶ EXTRA: TANGY SWEET 'N' SOUR SAUCE

6 boneless, skinless chicken breasts,
   or 10 boneless, skinless thighs,
   or 2 lb ground chicken
1/4 cup coconut flour
2 oz grated Parmesan cheese
2 oz grated cheddar cheese
1 large egg
1 tsp salt
1/2 tsp garlic powder
1/2 tsp pepper
olive oil, for frying

We love breaded chicken but hate the fuss of having raw eggs and crumbs all over the kitchen counter. What if you could have a recipe that had everything you love about nuggets and chicken burgers without the fuss of egg washes and breading?

The key to this recipe is pulsing the ingredients (even if you are using ground chicken) in the food processor or blender for a few minutes to create the nugget texture we are used to. You can make this recipe without a food processor, but the texture will not be the same.

Do not use pre-shredded cheese, as it is loaded with starches to keep it from sticking together in the bag.

This recipe is guaranteed to fool the kids; they will have no idea there is no batter.

Want to sauce these up? Whip up the tangy sweet 'n' sour sauce too, and take this recipe to a new level.

1. Preheat the oven to 400°F and line a baking sheet with aluminum foil and parchment paper.
2. Place all the ingredients in a food processor and pulse until the chicken is finely chopped and all the ingredients are combined. Measure out 1 tablespoon (or use a small ice cream scoop) for each nugget, or 3 to 4 tablespoons for each patty. Wet your hands with water to prevent sticking, then form and flatten the chicken into small nuggets and patties.
3. In a large sauté pan or heavy pot, heat the oil on a medium heat. The oil should cover the bottom of the pan and come to just past halfway up the chicken pieces.
4. Fry for 3 minutes per side. The nuggets will cook a little faster than the patties.
5. Remove from the oil and transfer to the prepared baking sheet tray to finish in the oven for 8 to 10 minutes.
6. Serve with tangy sweet 'n' sour sauce or try our BBQ sauces (page 171).

NOTE: 1/2 cup almond flour can be substituted for the coconut flour.

▶ **TANGY SWEET 'N' SOUR SAUCE**

1 cup apple cider or white vinegar
1 cup water
1/2 cup tomato sauce
1/2 cup powdered sweetener
1 tsp salt
1 tsp garlic powder
1/2 tsp dried parsley
1/2 tsp pepper
1/2 tsp Korean chili flakes or
   alternate heat
1/4 tsp dried thyme
1/4 tsp xanthan gum (optional)

Place all the ingredients in a saucepan and bring to a rapid boil. Whisk in a small amount (start with 1/8 teaspoon or less) of xanthan gum (if using) and let it boil for 3 to 5 minutes. Remove from the heat and wait 3 to 4 minutes to evaluate if more xanthan gum is needed. The sauce will thicken as it cools.

APPETIZERS AND SNACKS | 17

Cranberry Meatballs

❖ **VARIATION: JERK MEATBALLS**

FOR THE CRANBERRY COMPOTE
16 oz fresh or frozen cranberries
1 cup tomato sauce
1/2 cup powdered sweetener, or to taste
1/4 cup coconut sauce
1/4 cup chili garlic sauce
1/2 tsp garam masala
1/4 tsp salt
1/4 tsp nutmeg
1/4 cup apple cider or white vinegar

FOR THE MEATBALLS
2 lb ground pork, chicken, or turkey
1 lb ground beef
1/3 cup almond flour or crushed pork rinds
2 oz grated Parmesan cheese
1/8 cup powdered sweetener
1 large egg
1 medium onion, minced
3 large cloves garlic, minced
1 tsp paprika
1 tsp dried parsley
1 tsp salt
1 tsp dried summer savoury
1/2 tsp dried thyme
1/2 tsp pepper

These cranberry meatballs add a splash of colour to any potluck or family dinner. Batch-cook them: keep the sauce and meatballs separate and only combine the portion that you intend to use at a particular time.

These are a variation of sweet and sour meatballs, but the cranberry adds a festive flair to the dish. Garnish with a few sprigs of fresh parsley and it looks like Christmas on a plate.

Use crushed pork rinds instead of almond flour for a lower-carb option.

To prepare the cranberry compote
1. Cover the bottom of a medium saucepan with water and place all the ingredients except the vinegar in the pot. Simmer until the cranberries are soft and have burst open, about 10 to 12 minutes. Do not allow the sauce to reduce too much. Add extra water if it gets too thick. Remove from the heat and set aside to slightly cool.
2. Press the cranberry mixture through a vegetable mill or fine sieve to remove the solids. Discard solids that cannot be pushed through the mill.
3. Return the compote to the heat and add the vinegar. Simmer on a low heat for 20 to 30 minutes to allow the vinegar to mellow.
4. Set aside until the meatballs are ready.

To prepare the meatballs
1. Cover a baking sheet with aluminum foil and then a layer of parchment paper. The foil is for a quick clean up and the parchment paper keeps the meatballs from sticking.
2. Gently combine all the ingredients in a large bowl. Overmixing or compressing results in tough meatballs. Use splayed fingers and an upward motion to lift the ingredients instead of pressing the meat into the bowl.
3. Form into meatballs and place them on the prepared sheet. Use a mini ice cream scoop to create equal-sized meatballs and then finish them by rolling by hand.
4. Preheat the oven to 350°F and bake the meatballs until they reach an internal temperature of 165°F and are browned on the outside.
5. Spoon the cranberry compote over the meatballs and stir well to coat.

APPETIZERS AND SNACKS | 19

❖ **VARIATION: JERK MEATBALLS**
For a milder palate, reduce the spices.

To the meatball recipe above, add
1 tbsp chili powder
1 tsp allspice
1/2 tsp nutmeg
pinch of cloves

For the jerk sauce
1 cup water or broth
1/4 cup apple cider vinegar
1/4 cup coconut sauce
1/4 cup powdered sweetener
2 tbsp minced fresh ginger
1 tbsp fish sauce
2 tsp chili powder
2 tsp Dijon mustard
1 tsp minced jalapeño pepper (optional)
1/2 tsp cayenne pepper (optional)
1/2 tsp xanthan gum
pinch of nutmeg

Follow the instructions on page 18.

APPETIZERS AND SNACKS | 21

APPETIZERS AND SNACKS

Devilled Egg Unwich
❖ VARIATION: LOBSTER DEVILLED EGGS

12 large eggs
1/4 cup mayonnaise, or to taste
2 tbsp Dijon mustard
1 tsp hot sauce
1/2 cup sour cream
1 tsp salt, or to taste
1/2 tsp pepper, or to taste
1/2 tsp garlic powder
1/2 tsp onion powder

Optional
finely chopped fresh chives, for garnish
smoked paprika, for garnish

What's an *unwich*? It's all the fixins for a sandwich without the outside bread layer. You can make this into a killer egg sandwich or even pipe it into individual egg halves: our version is meant to be hassle- and guilt-free. Eating the egg mixture without the bread removes the excess carbs and belly bloat and replaces them with pure flavour and goodness.

Our devilled eggs aren't perfectly piped into the individual egg whites like the church-lady eggs we grew up with. Just chop them roughly, and mix in a bowl.

1. Place the cold eggs in a saucepan and cover with cold water. Place the saucepan on a high heat and bring the eggs to a rapid boil. Immediately turn off the heat and cover the saucepan with a lid. Let sit covered for 3 minutes for a runny egg and add 30-second increments for a firmer yolk.
2. Drain and run cool water over the eggs. Drain and repeat twice more with fresh water. This cools the shells while allowing the inner egg to stay warm. Peel the eggs with a spoon when the shells have cooled enough to handle.
3. Transfer the eggs to a medium mixing bowl and add the remaining ingredients except garnishes. Roughly chop to combine. Mash the egg for a smooth mix presentation or leave with a rough-chopped consistency. Transfer to a serving bowl. Sprinkle paprika and chives on the top and serve on a lettuce leaf, healthy bread, or crackers, or just spooned up.

✔ **TIP**
Peel the eggs right away; they are harder to peel after they have fully cooled. Crack the top of the egg with a knife or spoon and peel away the top portion of the shell. Slip a wet teaspoon between the edge of the egg and the shell and scoop the spoon all the way around the inside. The spoon will separate the shell from the egg, allowing it to be easily spooned out. Rinse the eggs one last time to remove any bits of shell.

❖ **VARIATION: LOBSTER DEVILLED EGGS**
Want to jazz up this recipe? Add 1 cup cooked lobster, 1 teaspoon finely chopped fresh chives, and 1/2 teaspoon dried tarragon to the mixture.

❖ **OTHER VARIATIONS**
2 tbsp blue cheese, for blue devilled eggs
1/2 avocado, mashed, for avo-devilled eggs
4 strips bacon, crumbled, for bacon-devilled eggs
4 oz smoked salmon on top, for salmon-devilled eggs
2 tbsp hot sauce, for Buffalo-devilled eggs

Dill-Lightful Wings WITH DILL AIOLI
➤ **EXTRA: PICKLING BRINE**

2 lb chicken wings
3 cups leftover dill pickle juice (or see recipe below)
1 tsp salt
1/2 tsp pepper
1 tsp garlic powder
2 tbsp melted butter

FOR THE DILL AIOLI
1 cup olive oil
1 large egg
1 tbsp minced dill pickles
1 1/2 tsp Dijon mustard
1 tsp minced fresh dill
1 tsp lemon juice
1 tsp apple cider vinegar
1 tsp salt and 1/2 tsp pepper, or to taste

Brining these wings boosts the juicy factor and adds a hint of extra flavour.

Don't get thrown off by the fancy name: an aioli is just a mayo made from olive oil. Ensure that the oil is hot before adding the wings. The hot oil quickly seals the outside of the wings and keeps them from being greasy. Alternatively, these wings can be baked at 350°F for 20 to 25 minutes. For crispier wings, a cooking time of 30 to 35 minutes is recommended.

Serve the wings with a little dill aioli on the side.

1. Combine the chicken wings and the pickle juice in a large sealable plastic bag and carefully remove the air from the bag. The wings need to be totally immersed in the brine. Alternatively, the chicken wings can be placed in the leftover brine in the pickle bottle, keeping in mind that they will displace some of the brine in the bottle. Work in the sink to avoid chicken-contaminated spillage.
2. Refrigerate to marinate for 6 to 10 hours.
3. Remove the wings from the brine and pat completely dry with paper towels. Extra water can cause the deep fryer oil to bubble over.
4. Deep-fry the wings at 350°F for 10 to 12 minutes or until they reach the desired doneness. Remove from the oil and drain.
5. In a large bowl, combine the butter, salt, pepper, and garlic powder. Toss the wings until coated and serve or use the dill aioli as a dipping sauce.

To prepare the dill aioli
1. Place all the ingredients in the cylinder of an immersion blender and allow the egg to sink to the bottom.
2. Place the immersion blender on the bottom and slowly raise it from the bottom to the top. The texture of the mixture changes as the aioli comes together.

➤ **PICKLING BRINE**

Make your own pickling brine! Combine 1 cup apple cider or white vinegar, 1/2 cup water, 1 tablespoon salt, 1 teaspoon powdered sweetener, 3 sprigs of fresh dill, and 1 clove garlic, smashed. Optional: add mustard seeds, peppercorns, bay leaves, and/or a pinch of cloves to taste.

Hickory Sticks
❖ WITH VARIATIONS

Hickory spice mix (below)
1 small to medium celeriac
lard, for frying

HICKORY SPICE MIX
2 tbsp salt
2 tbsp liquid smoke
1/2 tsp garlic powder
1/4 tsp paprika
1/4 tsp onion powder

Hickory sticks always take me back to my grandparents' shop and to a fellow who came into their old-style corner store every day for a chat, a bag of sticks, and a drink. I can see him now, standing around the old pot belly stove telling yarns to all who would listen, munching happily away on his bag of sticks. What I wouldn't give to be transported back in time to hang out with my grandparents and listen for a while.

For these hickory sticks, take it back to basics and make the seasoning spice mix a day or so in advance. These sticks can be baked in a 325°F oven for about 25 to 30 minutes but they won't be as crispy as the deep-fried version.

Always use a guard when slicing vegetables on a mandoline.

To prepare the hickory spice mix
1. Mix all the spice mix ingredients in a small bowl. It should resemble damp sand. Spread on a baking sheet.
2. Allow the mixture to dry at room temperature or in the oven at the lowest temperature until it is completely dry, like salt. Stir occasionally.
3. Store in a sealed glass bottle in a dry dark place.

To prepare the hickory sticks
1. Peel the celeriac, taking care to remove any dirt, then carefully slice into uniformly thin pieces or use the smallest setting on a mandoline. Stack the slices on a cutting board and neatly chop them into matchstick or julienne sticks that are about 1/8- to 1/4-inch-wide pieces.
2. Preheat the deep fryer to 325°F. Carefully add the matchsticks and cook until they are dark golden brown. Remove from the oil and place in a medium bowl. Toss with the premade hickory seasoning.

✔ **TIP**
Add 1 cup sour cream to turn these dry mixes into dips.

❖ **VARIATIONS**
Try these spice mixes on your next batch of sticks.

Bacon Mix
2 tsp powdered sweetener
2 tsp salt
2 tsp paprika
1/2 tsp garlic powder
1/2 tsp onion powder
1/4 tsp pepper
1/4 tsp ground sumac

Sour Cream and Onion Mix
1 tbsp heavy whipping cream powder
1 1/2 tsp onion powder
1 tsp salt
1 tsp garlic powder
1/2 tsp dried parsley

Ranch Mix
3 tsp heavy whipping cream powder
2 tsp dried tarragon or chives
2 tsp dried parsley
2 tsp dried dill
1 tsp garlic powder
1 tsp onion powder
1 tsp salt
1/2 tsp pepper

28 | APPETIZERS AND SNACKS

Lamb Kofta WITH POMEGRANATE JAM

1 1/2 tsp ground cumin
1 1/2 tsp toasted fennel seeds, crushed
1 tsp dried parsley
1 tsp salt
1 tsp pepper
1/2 tsp allspice
1 lb minced lamb, pork, or any other minced meat (or a combination of meats)
1/2 medium onion, minced
3 cloves garlic, minced and then puréed

2 tbsp oil, for frying
1/4 cup fresh parsley, to garnish

FOR THE POMEGRANATE JAM
seeds of 1 pomegranate
1 tbsp powdered sweetener
1 1/2 tbsp lemon juice
1/4 tsp ancho chili, or 1 tsp chili powder
1/8 cup water
pinch of salt

Think of a kofta as a grilled meatball, usually made from beef or lamb and seasoned with fragrant herbs and spices. Use pork or chicken to make these koftas, but the lamb adds a robust flavour that is definitely worth a try.

To prepare the kofta
1. Preheat the oven to 375°F and prepare a baking sheet with parchment paper. Set aside.
2. In a small mixing bowl, combine all the dry ingredients.
3. Place the lamb, dry ingredients, onion, and garlic in a large bowl and mix by hand until fully incorporated. Do not overmix. Separate into eight pieces and roll each into a kofta or cigar shape, about 1 by 2 inches. Place the formed koftas on the prepared sheet.
4. Place an oven-safe, medium sauté pan on a high heat. When the pan is hot, add the oil and then add the koftas in a clockwise fashion. Fry the koftas, only turning them when the outside has browned, about 1 to 2 minutes per side.
5. Transfer the sauté pan of koftas to the oven and bake until just cooked through, about 4 to 6 minutes, or to an internal temperature of 145°F.
6. Remove from the oven and set aside.

To prepare the pomegranate jam
Combine all the ingredients in a medium saucepan on a medium heat and simmer until the mixture is slightly reduced, about 8 to 10 minutes. Set aside.

To assemble
Plate the koftas and spoon about 1/2 teaspoon pomegranate jam on each kofta. Serve with fennel slaw, sautéed spinach, or steamed broccoli.

Pan-Seared Scallops WITH CHAMPAGNE REDUCTION

1 tsp ground cumin
1 tsp paprika
1 tsp garlic powder
1 tsp salt
1/2 tsp pepper
6 slices bacon, chopped in 1-inch squares
8 oz scallops, patted dry with paper towels
2 tbsp butter

FOR THE CHAMPAGNE SAUCE

2 green onions, white sections sliced
    (reserve the green tops for garnish)
1 tsp salt
1/2 tsp pepper
1 tsp coconut flour
1/4 cup champagne, white wine, or broth
1/8 cup apple cider or white vinegar
1/2 cup broth
2 tsp Dijon mustard
1 tsp dried thyme
1/2 cup whipping cream

FOR GARNISH

crumbled bacon
2 oz grated Parmesan cheese
green onion tops or fresh thyme

Scallops often get overcooked, which is unfortunate because it's truly the difference between soft, tender little delights and pieces of hard rubber.

The secret to this one-pot dish is a hot pan. The scallops need to be seared off hard or they will overcook inside before they are cooked to perfection on the outside.

Watch carefully. The side of the scallop turns from translucent to opaque as it cooks. Don't let it cook more than one-third of the way up on either side.

Turn this into a full meal by adding healthy pasta—such as konjac or shirataki noodles—and sautéed greens and other vegetables. The recipe also works with thin slices of pork, chicken, or beef instead of scallops.

To prepare the scallops
1. Whisk the spices together and sprinkle about half of it on the scallops.
2. Cook the bacon in a large sauté pan on a medium heat for about 5 minutes. Remove from the pan and set aside.
3. Remove all but about 2 tablespoons bacon fat from the pan and turn the heat to high. When the pan is hot, add the scallops, seasoned side down, around the edge of the pan in a clockwise fashion, keeping track of their order. Leave at least 1 inch between each scallop.
4. While the scallops are cooking, sprinkle the rest of the spice mix on the top of them.
5. Sear the scallops for about 2 minutes, or until a golden crust forms on the bottom.
6. Add the butter to the pan and then flip each scallop in the same order as they were placed in the pan. If you try to move the scallop (or any meat) and it is stuck on the pan, it means it is not ready to turn yet. Wait a while and try again instead of forcing it. Let the second side sear for about 45 seconds to 1 minute.
7. Remove the scallops from the pan and set aside. Reduce to medium heat.

To prepare the champagne sauce
1. To the same pan, add the onion and cook for about 3 minutes, stirring occasionally. Add the coconut flour, salt, and pepper to the pan and cook for 1 more minute or until the roux starts to turn a golden brown. Add the champagne and vinegar and cook for about 2 minutes to mellow the vinegar. Add the broth, Dijon mustard, and thyme, and continue cooking on a high heat for about 3 minutes, until the sauce starts to thicken.
2. Turn off the heat and stir in the cream.
3. Add the scallops and bacon. Stir to coat them with the sauce.
4. Garnish with crumbled bacon, fresh thyme, and grated Parmesan cheese.

❖ **VARIATION**

To turn this appetizer into a full meal, toss 1 teaspoon oil, 1/2 package of konjac pasta or an equivalent noodle replacement, 6 to 8 cherry tomatoes, and 3 to 4 cups fresh spinach (or equivalent frozen) in a sauté pan and cook until the spinach has wilted. Plate the seared scallops alongside the pasta.

APPETIZERS AND SNACKS | 31

Pork Belly WITH FIVE SPICE AND STICKY PHOENIX SAUCE
❖ VARIATION: ORANGE SPICE PORK BELLY

FOR THE FIVE-SPICE MIX
3 tbsp ground fennel
2 tsp pepper
2 tsp Ceylon cinnamon
1/2 tsp cloves
1/2 tsp ground ginger

FOR THE PORK BELLY
5 tbsp five-spice mix (recipe above)
2 tbsp salt
2 tsp pepper
1 lb pork belly

FOR THE STICKY PHOENIX SAUCE
1/3 cup coconut sauce
3/4 cup powdered sweetener
1/4 cup apple cider vinegar
4 cloves garlic, minced and mashed
1 bay leaf
1 tsp paprika
1/2 tsp salt
1/3 tsp cloves
1 tbsp Korean chili flakes
1 cup chicken or vegetable broth
1 tsp five-spice mix (recipe above)

This recipe was debuted at a recent restaurant takeover. The sauce for this dish was originally called Sticky Sauce.

It was a hectic meal service. One of our servers had called in sick and it was every person for themselves. We all had a set task list. You do this, I'll do that, and we'll all stay in our own lane and work quickly and efficiently.

The trouble arose with a typo in the sauce recipe. The spice component of the sauce was the culprit; it was way too big and it got followed to a tee.

The moral of the story? Never blindly follow a recipe. Typos happen, ovens and ingredients are different, and measuring spoons are not all created equal. A kitchen is a place where you must think on your feet for success. Use any recipe as a general guideline, and always use your common sense.

That Sticky Sauce was knock-your-socks-off HOT. It got fixed, but in the process, it also changed the name. Phoenix Sauce rose out of the (hot) ashes from that sticky sauce fail.

1. Whisk all the five-spice mix ingredients together. Set aside.
2. Preheat the oven to 350°F.
3. Score the pork belly fat by cutting diagonally at 1/4- to 1/2-inch intervals, cutting through the fat but not into the meat. Rub the pork belly with the spice rub, ensuring that the rub is pushed into the cuts.
4. Place the pork belly, fat side up, in a large roasting pan. Cover tightly with foil and roast for 90 minutes.
5. While the pork is roasting, make the sticky phoenix sauce.
6. After 90 minutes, increase the oven temperature to 400°F and remove the foil. Continue roasting for 45 minutes, or until the pork is tender on the inside and crisp on the outside. If necessary, switch to the broil setting and place the pork under the grill, without burning, until the top is crisp. Watch carefully that the pork does not burn.
7. Remove from the oven and rest for 20 minutes. Do not tent or cover. After 20 minutes, cut the pork in 2- by 2-inch pieces and set aside. To turn this into a full meal, increase the size of the meat pieces to 2 by 4 inches per serving and serve with Fennel Slaw (page 106).

To prepare the sticky phoenix sauce
Place all the ingredients in a medium saucepan on a low-medium heat. Cook and reduce for 15 to 16 minutes until the sauce is glossy and has a loose caramel consistency. Discard the bay leaf.

To serve
Place 1 to 2 tablespoons sauce in the base of each plate, then place a piece of pork belly on top of it. Spoon a little sauce on the pork belly and serve.

APPETIZERS AND SNACKS | 33

❖ **VARIATION: ORANGE SPICE PORK BELLY**
Substitute this orange spice glaze for the sticky phoenix sauce.

1/4 cup apple cider vinegar, to deglaze the pan
1/2 cup dry white wine
1/2 cup water
1/4 cup powdered sweetener
2 tbsp coconut sauce
1 tsp salt
3 oz fresh ginger, finely grated
2 cloves garlic, minced
1 carrot, cut in matchsticks
1/2 tsp fennel seed, crushed
1/2 tsp Ceylon cinnamon
1/2 tsp food-grade orange oil
1/2 tsp Korean chili flakes
zest of 1 orange

Follow the instructions on page 32.

Warm Bacon Dip

8 oz cream cheese, at room temperature
1/2 cup sour cream or mayonnaise
1/2 cup grated cheddar
  or any sharp cheese
8 slices bacon, cooked and crumbled
1/2 cup sliced green onion
2 cloves garlic, minced and smashed
2 tsp dried parsley,
  or 1/4 cup chopped fresh parsley
1 tsp fish sauce
1 tsp hot sauce (optional)
1 tsp paprika
1/2 tsp Korean chili flakes

We couldn't justify having a book about comfort food without including this recipe. It's loaded with bacon and cream cheese and is so ooey gooey that it almost personifies comfort food all on its own.

This dip is easy to customize. Remove the bacon and add various flavour components to suit your family's tastes. It is delicious served hot or cold.

1. Preheat the oven to 400°F and grease a medium baking dish.
2. Combine all the ingredients and spoon into the prepared dish. Bake for 20 minutes or until the cheese is melted and bubbly.
3. Serve with crackers, vegetables, or healthy breadsticks.

✔ **TIP**

Expecting company? Bake this dip in individual ramekin dishes. For another flavour, replace the bacon with 10 ounces crab meat or try Spinach Dip (page 292). More flavour ideas: how about baked asparagus? Buffalo style? Black olive? Broccoli cheese? Chipotle Mexican? Creamy onion? Taco?

Breakfast and Brunch

The Science of Eggs ...

Avo BLT Chaffle
Baked Cinnamon French Toast
Bell Pepper Egg Rings
Blueberry Pancakes
Fish Cakes Eggs Benny
Greek Omelette
Ham, Mushroom, and Tomato Hash
    with Sunny-Side-Up Eggs
Mushroom Pie
Quiche Lorraine
Salsa Egg Skillet

The debate over whether to consume them raw or cooked is an interesting one.

In raw eggs, a protein called avidin (found in the egg white) binds to biotin in the yolk, making it unavailable for your body to use. So, the egg yolk is best eaten raw to avail of all the yummy goodness that egg yolk has to offer.

However, when these same eggs are cooked, the heat structurally changes avidin, making it less effective at binding to biotin. So, avidin is generally inactivated when cooked, which in turn makes the biotin in the yolk fully available for absorption by the body. Avidin is also an antinutrient, which means it can bind to other foods and prevent absorption of those nutrients as well.

So, putting it in simplified terms, the protein and nutrients from the egg are more digestible (94% versus 55-64%) when the whites are heated. However, all the nutrients found in egg yolks are more bioavailable when raw. Therein lies the dilemma. The nutrients in egg whites are most bioavailable when cooked; in yolks, when raw.

For this reason, when scrambling eggs, reserve half the yolks; quickly fold in the reserved eggs, with a little butter, just as the heat is turned off.

Avo BLT Chaffle

FOR THE AVO MASH

1 ripe avocado, peeled and mashed
1 tbsp lemon juice
1 clove garlic, mashed, or 1 tsp garlic powder
1/2 tsp salt
1/2 tsp pepper
pinch of Korean chili flakes

FOR THE CHAFFLE

2 large eggs
8 oz grated cheddar cheese
1/4 tsp cream of tartar

TO ASSEMBLE

strips of bacon, cooked
lettuce
tomato, sliced
salt and pepper, to taste

Chaffles—cheese and egg mixed and cooked in a mini waffle maker—are easy and delicious. This recipe combines avo toast with a BLT with a chaffle for an out-of-the-world refreshing and satisfying breakfast. The creamy avo mash eliminates the need for mayonnaise.

Make these chaffles ahead of time. Then mash the avocado and assemble the fixings just before eating. Chaffles are good hot, at room temperature, or even cold.

Be patient with yourself the first time you make these. There's a learning curve in figuring out how much batter to put in the waffle maker and how long to cook them.

To prepare the avo mash
Mash all the ingredients together in a small bowl and set aside.

To prepare the chaffles
1. Spray the mini waffle maker with olive or avocado oil and then preheat until ready.
2. In a small bowl, combine all the chaffle ingredients. Spoon 1/4 cup batter into the mini waffle maker and spread a thin layer to fill to the edges. The batter expands as it cooks.
3. Close the lid and allow to cook for 5 to 7 minutes; at 5 minutes, the chaffles will be cooked but still blonde; closer to 7 minutes gives the traditional waffle grate marks.
4. Remove the chaffle and place it on a cooling rack. Repeat the process for any remaining batter.

To assemble
Spoon about 3 tablespoons avo mash on a chaffle. Cover with two pieces of bacon, tomato slices, lettuce, and another chaffle. Season with salt and pepper.

Breakfast and Brunch | 39

Baked Cinnamon French Toast

8 oz Soured Dough Bread (page 290),
  or any healthy bread, cubed
1/2 cup butter
3/4 cup powdered sweetener,
  or to taste
1 1/2 tsp Ceylon cinnamon
1/4 tsp nutmeg
1/4 tsp ground cardamom
1/4 tsp salt

FOR THE CUSTARD

6 large eggs
1 1/4 cups whipping cream, diluted with
  3/4 cup water
2 tsp pure vanilla extract
1 tsp Ceylon cinnamon

FOR THE TOPPING

2 tsp Ceylon cinnamon
1 tbsp brown sweetener, or
  equivalent powdered white

Before I discovered the time-saving joys of batch cooking, I made French toast a few pieces at a time on demand. This usually made for a hectic morning at our place. These days I increase the quantity and put a few cooked servings in the freezer for quick and easy meals down the road. Making this dish the night before and refrigerating it saves time and also increases the flavour of the toast.

The smaller the bread cubes, the more saucy and flavourful the final dish will be; the bigger the cube, the more the flavour is diluted.

1. Grease a 13- by 9-inch oven-safe baking dish with Bakers Magic (Pan) Release (page 273). Set aside.
2. In a large saucepan, melt the butter on a low-medium heat. Stir in the sweetener and spices until everything dissolves and the butter mixture is smooth. Remove from the heat and allow to cool slightly.
3. Add the bread cubes to the cooled butter mixture and stir to incorporate. Spread the cubes in the prepared baking pan.
4. In a medium bowl, whisk together the eggs, milk, vanilla, and cinnamon. Pour the egg mixture over the bread cubes, ensuring that all the pieces are covered. Refrigerate overnight or at least 1 hour to allow the flavours to infuse the bread.
5. Preheat the oven to 400°F.
6. Whisk the topping ingredients together. Remove the bread cubes from the refrigerator and sprinkle with the topping. Bake for 35 to 40 minutes until the top is golden brown. Remove from the oven and sprinkle with powdered sweetener if using.

✔ **TIP**

To amp up this recipe, toss a handful of blueberries or pecans into the unbaked French toast or drizzle 1/4 cup Maple Syrup Substitute (page 283) over the topping at the baking midway mark.

Bell Pepper Egg Rings

1/2 tsp salt
1/2 tsp dried parsley
1/2 tsp onion powder
1/4 tsp pepper
2 tbsp oil
3 bell pepper rings, 1/4 to 1/3 inch thick
2 tbsp crumbled precooked bacon
3 cherry tomatoes, thinly sliced
1 clove garlic, minced and mashed, or 1/2 tsp garlic powder
3 medium eggs
fresh chives or parsley, to garnish

This recipe began as a mission to create a quick and easy breakfast for my father. There I was hunting around in the refrigerator trying to rummage up something to keep Dad's belly satisfied and like a master chef contestant on a timed pantry visit, I grabbed a pepper, a couple of eggs, and some spices.

The first thing I did was cut the peppers into slices. As I chopped, I noticed that the eggs kept rolling around the countertop. I laid one in each of the pepper rings to keep them from moving around. Instantly, my mind made the connection. Do the same thing in the pan. And a recipe was born.

Feel free to change up the bacon for another meat and switch out the spices to suit your preferences. Use the dry mixes (page 166) to create different flavours for this and all other dishes.

1. Mix the seasonings in a small bowl.
2. Heat the oil in a large non-stick sauté pan on a medium heat. Add the bell pepper rings. Cook for 2 to 3 minutes on each side. The peppers should be soft but not starting to brown. Add the bacon, tomato, and garlic to each ring. Crack an egg in each bell pepper ring and sprinkle with the seasonings. Lower the heat to the lowest setting and cover the pan with a lid.
3. Keep the lid on for at least 2 minutes for a sunny-side-up egg, about 5 minutes for a soft yolk, and closer to 10 minutes for a harder yolk.
4. Transfer the rings to a plate. Garnish and serve.

Blueberry Pancakes

❖ **VARIATION: PUMPKIN PANCAKES**

1 cup almond flour
1 tbsp powdered sweetener
1 tbsp egg white powder
1/2 tsp cream of tartar
1/4 tsp baking soda
1/4 tsp xanthan gum
pinch of salt
2 large eggs
1/4–1/2 cup whipping cream
1 tsp pure vanilla extract
1/2 cup blueberries, fresh or frozen
oil, for frying

No breakfast food takes me back in time faster than a plate of blueberry pancakes. The very idea of them transports me back home, watching Mom dollop batter into a pan.

Blueberries can be replaced with pumpkin spice, other berries, chocolate chips, peanut butter, or even cooked bacon.

Always add liquids in increments—if the batter needs to be thinned, add more liquid.

1. Combine the dry ingredients in a medium mixing bowl. Add the eggs, cream, and vanilla and whisk until a thick batter forms. Fold in the blueberries.
2. Heat the oil in a sauté pan on a medium-high heat. When the oil is hot, spoon 1/4 cup batter into the pan for each pancake. Larger pancakes are harder to flip.
3. Reduce the heat to low and cover the pan to allow the centre of the pancake to cook slowly.
4. Check the pancakes at about 2 to 3 minutes. Shake the pan lightly to determine if they have firmed up or need a minute longer. Flip the pancake after 3 to 5 minutes, or when the surface of the pancake is full of bubbles. Cook for about 1 minute on the other side.
5. Remove the pancakes from the pan and turn the heat back up to medium high and repeat the process for more pancakes.

NOTE: This recipe can be made in a waffle maker. Frozen berries make this batter wetter and colour the batter. Reduce the liquid if using frozen berries.

❖ **VARIATION: PUMPKIN PANCAKES**

Omit the berries and whipping cream. Instead add 1/2 cup pure pumpkin puree, 1 1/2 teaspoons Ceylon cinnamon, 1/2 teaspoon allspice, 1/4 teaspoon ground cardamom, and 1/4 teaspoon ground ginger to the pancakes. Follow the cooking instructions above.

Fish Cakes Eggs Benny

FOR THE FISH CAKES

1/4 cup almond flour
1/8 cup coconut flour
1 tsp dried summer savoury
1/2 tsp dried tarragon
　or parsley or a combination
1/2 tsp pepper
1 cup boiled and mashed celeriac
1 lb boneless, skinless salted cod,
　boiled and cooled
1/4 cup butter
1 shallot, minced
2 cloves garlic, minced
2 large eggs
2 tbsp oil, for the pan
2 tbsp butter, for the flip

FOR THE EGGS

3 large eggs
2 tbsp white vinegar
1 tsp salt

Eggs Benny can seem a little intimidating at first, but it really is simple.

Hollandaise is one of the mother sauces that forms the foundation of French cooking—don't fear it.

This breakfast will work best on a lazy weekend morning when you have a set of extra hands in the kitchen. Getting the timing for the hollandaise and the poached egg right can be challenging, so opt for the buddy system your first time.

Make the fish cakes ahead of time. Then move on to the next elements as the cakes are resting on a side plate, or in the pan which has been removed from the heat.

This recipe makes six fish cakes; you may opt to freeze three for future use.

To prepare the fish cakes

1. Preheat the oven to 400°F. Line a baking sheet with aluminum foil and parchment paper. Set aside.
2. Place the dry ingredients in a small bowl and whisk.
3. Combine all the ingredients in a large bowl and assemble into cakes.
4. Drizzle the oil on the prepared pan, place the fish cakes on the pan, and bake for 30 minutes.
5. Remove the fish cakes from the oven and dot the butter all over the hot pan. Let it melt onto the bottom of the cakes, then flip them over, ensuring that both sides have a thin coating of butter. Bake for another 20 to 25 minutes or until the fish cakes are cooked through and golden brown on the outside.

To prepare the eggs

1. Carefully break the eggs into a small bowl. Do not break the yolks.
2. Boil the water and vinegar in a large pot. When it is boiling, stir the water in a circular motion. Carefully drop each egg into the hot water, spacing them in the circular flow. Keep the water moving.
3. The cooking times depend on the egg size. For large eggs:
　Soft: 3 minutes, a runny yolk and soft white.
　Medium: 5 minutes, a yolk that is a bit more set.
　Hard: 6 minutes, a firm yolk and white.
4. Use a slotted spoon to lift each egg from the water.

FOR THE HOLLANDAISE SAUCE

3 large egg yolks
1 tbsp lemon juice or vinegar
1 tsp Dijon mustard
1/2 tsp salt
pinch of paprika
1/2 cup hot melted butter

FOR GARNISH

3 thick slices of ham, precooked (optional)
paprika
green onion, chopped

To prepare the hollandaise sauce
Place all the ingredients except the butter in a bowl and use an immersion blender to combine. Slowly drizzle in the hot butter while mixing the sauce.

To assemble
Plate the ham on the bottom, then a fish cake, and add the poached egg and the hollandaise sauce. Garnish with a sprinkle of paprika and chopped green onion.

NOTE: If using fresh (not salted or cured) fish, add 1 teaspoon salt to the fish cakes.

✔ **TIP**
Do not add milk or butter to the celeriac mash. Liquids make the fish cakes too runny.

48 | BREAKFAST AND BRUNCH

Greek Omelette

FILLINGS

1 tbsp oil
2/3 cup roughly chopped fresh spinach
2 tbsp diced red onion or shallots
1/4 cup cherry tomatoes, seeded and chopped
1/4 cup black olives, pitted and sliced
1 clove garlic, minced and smashed

FOR THE OMELETTE

1 tsp dried parsley, or 1 sprig of fresh parsley, chopped
1 tsp minced fresh thyme or dill
1 tsp salt
1/2 tsp pepper
1/2 tsp Korean chili flakes (optional)
2 tbsp oil
6 large eggs, beaten
2 oz crumbled feta cheese

Omelettes are a practice-makes-perfect dish. It takes many trials to learn how to manoeuvre the eggs and set up the bottom of an omelette to receive the fillings. Flipping the omelette is another pressure point. But even if the omelette flops visually, it will still taste good — consider it a fancy scrambled egg dish. And if a perfect Greek omelette happens, let it be a pleasant surprise!

Substitute Greek-inspired fillings with any precooked fillings.

1. Sauté all the fillings to the desired doneness and set aside.
2. Whisk the eggs in a small mixing bowl.
3. Pour the oil into a medium sauté pan on a medium-high heat. When the pan is hot, add the eggs and immediately season with salt and pepper. Use a small spatula to keep the eggs moving in the pan; do not let the eggs set on the bottom of the pan just yet.
4. After about 30 to 45 seconds, flatten the surface of the egg with a spatula, creating a solid layer of cooked egg. Add the fillings and cheese in a line down the centre of the omelette. Cover and turn off the heat for 30 seconds.
5. With the spatula, lift one edge of the omelette away and fold one edge (about one-third) of the omelette over onto itself in the pan. This portion may crack. Turn off the heat.
6. Tilt the pan to roll the omelette onto the plate, seam side down.

BREAKFAST AND BRUNCH | 51

Ham, Mushroom, and Tomato Hash
WITH SUNNY-SIDE-UP EGGS

FOR THE HASH

1 medium onion, diced

4-6 mushrooms, sliced

2 cloves garlic, peeled and minced

1 tsp dried parsley, or a handful of fresh parsley, chopped

1/2 tsp pepper

1 cup roughly chopped fresh spinach or alternate greens

8 oz cooked ham (or alternate meat), roughly diced

1 large tomato, chopped

FOR THE EGGS

oil, for cooking

4 large eggs

1 tsp salt and 1/2 tsp pepper, or to taste

Breakfast is a relaxed affair at our home. It can be a planned-ahead-of-time or a let's-see-what's-in-the-fridge-today event. The latter is definitely my favourite—and this recipe is ideal for such mornings.

To prepare the hash
1. Place the oil in a medium sauté pan on a medium heat. When it is hot, add the onion and sauté for 3 to 4 minutes, or until the onion is slightly translucent. Add the mushrooms, garlic, and spices and cook for 2 minutes. Add the ham, spinach, and tomato and cook for 2 to 3 minutes, or until the spinach has wilted.
2. While the spinach wilts, cook the eggs.

To prepare the eggs
1. Crack the eggs into a medium bowl, taking care not to break the yolks.
2. Pour the oil into a large sauté pan on a medium heat. When the oil is hot, gently drop the eggs, one by one, into the pan, spacing them out. Season the eggs with salt and pepper and cover.
3. Reduce the heat to low and cook for approximately 3 minutes for a runny yolk (about 5 minutes for a firmer yolk), or until the eggs are cooked.
4. When the eggs are almost cooked, plate the hash. Place the eggs alongside the hash and serve.

NOTE: Try serving the eggs on top of the hash so that the yolks run down over it and add to the overall flavour. Keep the eggs covered while cooking them. Opening the lid causes the heat to escape. Use a pan with a glass lid to see what is going on in the pan.

Mushroom Pie

FOR THE CRUST
(MAKES 2 MEDIUM CRUSTS)

16 oz grated mozzarella cheese
1/2 tsp dried oregano
1/4 tsp dried basil
1 tsp garlic powder
1/2 tsp onion powder
1/2 tsp xanthan gum
1 cup powdered pork rinds (use a blender), or 1 cup almond flour
2 large eggs

FILLINGS/TOPPINGS

2 tbsp butter or oil
1 lb assorted fresh mushrooms (cremini, chanterelles, white or brown button), thinly sliced and chopped
1/2 medium onion, thinly sliced
3-4 cloves garlic, minced
1 tsp ground cumin
1 tsp ground ginger
1 tsp salt
1/2 tsp dried thyme
1/2 tsp pepper
1/2 tsp ground coriander
1/2 tsp garam masala
1/4 tsp Ceylon cinnamon
1/4 tsp nutmeg
2 oz goat cheese

Mushrooms and garlic are a match made in culinary heaven. Mushrooms are full of earthy woodsy flavour and garlic brings their flavour to a whole new dimension.

This crust can be shaped into a pie crust or laid out pizza-style. The latter is the best option if you're trying to keep carb levels low; mushrooms are a little higher in carbs than most other vegetables, so a thin layer of mushrooms on the flat-style pizza pie will be more than enough.

Making this pizza as a pie in a cast-iron pan allows you to pile the mushrooms and goat cheese high in the pan, deep-dish style, to get maximum filling for every bite.

To prepare the crust
1. Preheat the oven to 350°F.
2. Tear off two large (finished crust size) pieces of parchment paper.
3. Place the grated mozzarella cheese in a large mixing bowl and set aside.
4. In a medium mixing bowl, combine the spices and pork rinds. Sprinkle this mixture into the grated mozzarella and toss to coat the cheese.
5. Next, incorporate the egg into the dough by hand and form into a ball.
6. Place the dough between two pieces of parchment paper and use a rolling pin to roll out the dough, or form the crust by hand.

For a pizza-type crust
1. Leaving both parchment sheets in place, place the crust on a pizza pan and bake it for 10 minutes, then flip (use the double sheets of parchment to help with flipping) and bake for another 10 minutes.
2. The crust is now ready for toppings.

For a pie-type crust
1. Follow the instructions for the pie crust on page 56.
2. Set the baked pie crust aside to slightly cool while working on the filling.

To prepare the filling/topping
1. Add the oil to a medium sauté pan on a medium-high heat.
2. When the oil is hot, add the onions and cook for 3 to 5 minutes.
3. Add the mushrooms and cook for 3 to 5 minutes more.
4. Add about 1/4 cup water to the pan and then add the garlic and spices directly into the water. This helps to evenly distribute the spices.
5. Let the mushroom mixture continue to cook until the water has cooked off, usually about 2 to 3 minutes. The finished mushroom mixture should be mostly dry with no water or juice at the bottom of the pan. Excess water makes the dough soggy.
6. Remove the mushroom mixture from the heat and add to the pizza base.
7. Crumble the goat cheese on top of the mushrooms.
8. Bake the pie for 10 minutes. Use a culinary torch to slightly char the cheese when it comes out of the oven, as goat cheese softens but does not melt as other cheeses do.

NOTE: Cover any leftover dough with plastic wrap and freeze for future use.

BREAKFAST AND BRUNCH | 55

Quiche Lorraine

**FOR THE CRUST
(MAKES 2 MEDIUM CRUSTS)**

3 cups almond flour
1/4 cup coconut flour
2 tbsp powdered sweetener
1/2 tsp xanthan gum
1/4 tsp salt
1/2 cup butter, cut in small chunks
1 large egg

FOR THE QUICHE FILLING

6 large eggs plus 2 large egg yolks
1 cup whipping cream
2 tsp dried parsley
1 tsp salt
1/2 tsp pepper
6-8 slices thick bacon, cooked, roughly chopped
2 oz grated Swiss, mozzarella, or Gruyère cheese
1/4 cup diced onion, caramelized in the bacon fat
1/4 tsp nutmeg

Quiche is a pastry crust filled with savoury custard and cheese, meat, seafood, or vegetables. The best-known variant is quiche Lorraine, which traditionally contains eggs, bacon, and cream.

We use different fillings every time we make a quiche. This healthified quiche recipe can be made dozens of ways—swap out veggies, meat, and spices as desired.

Blind-baking is the key to this recipe: prebake the pie crust and get it ready to receive the filling. Skipping this step will likely result in a soggy crust. This recipe makes 2 9-inch pie crusts.

This is a lovely breakfast for the weekend or a special family gathering.

To prepare the crust
1. In a medium mixing bowl, combine the dry ingredients.
2. Cut in the butter with a pastry cutter or a fork. Add the egg and use the cutter to thoroughly combine all the ingredients. Wrap the dough in plastic wrap and refrigerate for 1 hour to 3 days.
3. Roll out the dough between two sheets of parchment paper.
4. Grease a pie plate with butter and remove one sheet of parchment paper. Place the dough on a baking sheet, uncovered side up. Next, place the pie plate face down over the top. Quickly flip the tray and the pie plate, turning the whole thing upside down.
5. With the top sheet of parchment paper still in place, allow the dough to fall into the pie plate. Trim the edge of the crust to about 1 inch bigger than the pie plate. Tuck the excess dough under the edge of the crust to create a thicker edge. Either scallop the pie edge using thumb and forefinger or leave it as it is. Refrigerate the unbaked crust for 15 minutes.
6. Preheat the oven to 350°F.
7. Place pie weights, dried rice, or beans on top of the parchment paper and blind-bake the crust for 10 to 12 minutes. Remove the weights and the top sheet of parchment paper by gathering the edge of the parchment paper together and lift it like a sack. Reduce the oven heat to 300°F and bake the crust for 10 minutes or until it is cooked in the centre. It is now ready to be filled.

To prepare the quiche filling
1. In a medium bowl, whisk the egg and spices.
2. Place half the bacon in a layer on the precooked crust, followed by half the cheese and half the onion. Repeat. Pour the egg on the layers and bake for about 45 minutes or until the quiche is lightly browned.
3. Let stand for about 10 minutes to slightly cool before serving.

NOTE: Cover the edges of the pie crust with aluminum foil if it starts to brown too much. When the solid ingredients are placed in the crust, it will seem as if the pie is full and the egg-cream mixture is too much for the chosen plate. The egg, however, seeps into the unfilled cracks.

Salsa Egg Skillet

FOR THE SALSA

1 14-oz can tomatoes
1/2 medium onion, diced
1/2 cup diced peppers
1 large jalapeño pepper, seeded and minced
2 tbsp apple cider or white vinegar
1 tbsp powdered sweetener
1 1/2 tsp ground cumin
1 tsp dried parsley
1 tsp salt
1/2 tsp dried oregano
1/2 tsp ground coriander

FOR THE EGGS

1 tbsp oil
1/3 bell pepper, cut in thick slices
1 1/2 cups fresh spinach
1 tsp salt
1/2 tsp pepper
1/2 tsp ground cumin
1/4 tsp ground coriander
4 large eggs, at room temperature
1/3 cup salsa
cheddar cheese, grated, for garnish

This recipe is a combination of farm-fresh eggs (if available), vegetables, and salsa.

This dish is inspired by shakshuka, a popular dish in North Africa and the Middle East. But in our house, we just call it delicious.

To prepare the salsa
Put all the ingredients in a large pot and stir well. Bring to a boil, then reduce to a simmer and cook for about 1 hour.

To prepare the eggs
Place the oil in a medium skillet on a low-medium heat and sauté the peppers for 3 minutes. Add the spices and spinach and sauté until the spinach has wilted. Add a little water to help wilt the spinach. Add the eggs, being careful not to break the yolks. Add the salsa, spooning it around the eggs. Cover, reduce the heat to low, and cook for 5 to 10 minutes, depending on the yolk preference.

Soups and Stews

Comfort in a Bowl...

Celeriac, Leek, and Bacon Soup
Chicken and Ginger Noodle Bowl
Cream of Chicken Soup
Fennel Soup
Italian Wedding Soup
Jalapeño Popper Soup
Portuguese Fish Stew
Roasted Green Tomato Soup
Stinging Nettle Soup
Taco Soup
White Asparagus (Spargel) Soup

Some say that the concept of soups and stews is as old as cooking itself. Even before clay pottery, ancient soup makers could have dug a pit lined with animal skins or tree bark and filled this pit with water, meat, and bones and then dropped in some hot rocks. Unfortunately, these natural materials did not work well to preserve history, so we're left wondering.

These methods would have provided easily digestible, nutritious sustenance to our ancestors. I'm also sure that somewhere early on, somebody realized that stretching the broth or adding liquid to make more soup was an easy way to feed the masses.

Advances in the world of pottery would have made soups even more popular. Over time, it would have been noticed that the herbs and spices originally used as medicine to cure illness and ailments had the added benefit of flavouring the pot.

In our world of Instant Pots, soups are still associated with Nan's kitchen. They are a pick-me-up when we're feeling poorly or a warm-up on a cold day. Soups, stews, and broths are comfort foods. Go ahead and indulge.

Celeriac, Leek, and Bacon Soup

2 tbsp butter or oil

2 large leeks, white and light green parts only, roughly chopped, about 2-3 cups

1 medium celeriac, chopped in 1/2-inch pieces

3 cloves garlic, minced and puréed

4 cups chicken or vegetable broth

1 bay leaf

3 sprigs fresh thyme, bundled, or 1 tsp dried thyme

1 tsp dried parsley

1 tsp salt

1/2 tsp pepper

1/4 tsp nutmeg

4 strips bacon, cooked crispy and minced (plus more to garnish)

1/2 cup whipping cream

fresh chives or parsley, finely chopped, for garnish

This delicately spiced soup with a mild leek flavour is made creamy by adding celeriac or celery root. The celeriac can be substituted with any healthy potato replacement such as daikon, cauliflower, or jicama. The carb count depends on the substitute.

Use only the white and light green portions of the leeks. Keep the darker greens for bone broth. Keep a container in the freezer for this purpose.

This soup freezes well. If freezing this soup, add the cream after thawing and reheating the soup.

1. Place the butter in a large stockpot on a medium heat. Add the leeks, celeriac, and garlic, and sauté, allowing the leeks to sweat and the celeriac to soften for about 10 minutes. Lower the temperature slightly if the mixture browns. Keep stirring the vegetables. Add the broth, bay leaf, spices, and bacon and allow the mixture to come to a boil. Cover and simmer for about 15 to 20 minutes, or until the celeriac is very soft. Remove the bay leaf and thyme sprig, if bundled, then set the soup aside to slightly cool.
2. Purée the soup with an immersion blender until smooth. Add the whipping cream and return it to a simmer. Adjust the seasoning with salt and pepper. Garnish with extra bacon and fresh parsley or chives.

NOTE: Add 1/2 to 1 teaspoon Korean chili flakes (to taste) for extra spiciness. Add 1 medium onion, diced, with the leeks, for extra onion flavour. If the soup is too thin, simmer until it has thickened; if too thick, add water or broth to the desired consistency.

Chicken and Ginger Noodle Bowl

FOR THE CHICKEN

2 tbsp olive oil

3 boneless, skinless chicken breasts or 8 thighs

1 tsp salt

1 tsp ground ginger

1 tsp garlic powder

1/2 tsp pepper

FOR THE BROTH

2 tbsp oil

1 medium onion, thinly sliced

1 fennel bulb, sliced

6 oz piece of ginger, sliced in thin discs

4 cloves garlic, minced and mashed

1 stalk of lemongrass, sliced in thin strips

2 tsp salt

1 tsp powdered sweetener

2 tsp fennel seeds, crushed

1 tsp Ceylon cinnamon

1 tsp ground coriander

1/2 tsp ground ginger

1/2 tsp ground cardamom

1/2 tsp pepper

1 tbsp fish sauce

8 cups chicken broth

This was inspired by an authentic chicken ginger pho that we tried while abroad years ago.

Pho is usually pronounced as *phuh* in English, but a better approximation would be *feu* as pronounced in French. This traditional Vietnamese soup originated during the French colonial occupation of Vietnam. It was most likely an adaptation of the French one-pot beef and vegetable stew pot-au-feu. Pho gained popularity in the outside world when many fled the country after the Vietnam war. Pho dishes from northern Vietnam are usually salty, while the southern version is characterized by sweeter notes. But it is always rich in broth and full of noodles, meat, vegetables, and aromatics.

It's a fun dish to serve to guests as a build-your-own soup bowl bar.

To prepare the chicken

1. Preheat the oven to 350°F and line a baking sheet with parchment paper.
2. Place the chicken on the baking sheet and drizzle the oil on the top and season with the salt, ginger, garlic, and pepper. Bake until the chicken has cooked through to an internal temperature of 165°F. Let cool before cutting.

To prepare the broth

1. While the chicken is cooking, place the oil, onion, fennel, and ginger in a large sauté pan and gently cook until the onion starts to caramelize, about 4 to 5 minutes. Add the garlic and lemongrass and cook for 2 to 3 minutes. Add the sweetener and spices and cook for 2 to 3 minutes. Remove the fennel slices and set aside with the garnish, then add the fish sauce and chicken broth. Cover with a lid and gently simmer for about 15 minutes.
2. While the broth is simmering, follow the cooking instructions for the package of noodles, if using. Drain and divide the noodles between serving bowls.
3. Slice the chicken.
4. Ladle the broth on the noodles.
5. Place the chicken, toppings, and broth bowls on the table.
6. Plate the dish with choice of garnish and a lime wedge to squeeze over.

NOTE: Enoki can be gently cooked or added raw and gently warmed in the hot broth in the bowl. Nupasta, spiralized vegetable noodles, hearts of palm, or any healthy noodle can be used. If using shirataki or konjac noodles, rinse well and cut the noodles in half.

SUGGESTED TOPPINGS

1 package of shirataki noodles, or another healthy noodle

6 large soft-boiled eggs, halved

3 green onions, finely sliced on the diagonal

enoki mushrooms, or any mushrooms, sliced thin and ends trimmed

1 carrot, cut in matchsticks

1 cup mung bean sprouts

1 small bunch of Thai basil, coriander, or cilantro

1 lime, in wedges

hoisin-style sauce (see below)

hot sauce

HOISIN-STYLE SAUCE

1 tsp salt

1 tsp coconut flour

1/2 tsp Korean chili flakes

1/2 cup powdered sweetener

1/2 tsp ground cardamom

1/2 tsp Ceylon cinnamon

1/2 tsp pepper

1/4 tsp ground coriander

1/4 tsp xanthan gum

pinch of nutmeg

1 tbsp olive oil

2 cloves garlic, minced

2 tbsp almond butter

2 tbsp white vinegar

1 cup water

1/4 cup coconut sauce

To prepare the hoisin-style sauce

1. Whisk all the dry ingredients and set aside.
2. Put the oil in a sauté pan on a medium heat. Add the garlic and cook for 2 to 3 minutes.
3. Add the remaining ingredients and reduce the heat to a simmer for 10 minutes, stirring often.
4. Let cool. Blend with an immersion blender for a smooth sauce.

Cream of Chicken Soup

▶ OPTIONAL: CHICKEN SCRATCHINS

2 tbsp oil
4-6 boneless, skinless chicken thighs, cut in 1-inch chunks
1 tsp salt
1/2 tsp pepper
2 tbsp oil or butter
1 medium onion, diced
2 carrots, peeled and diced
2 stalks celery, diced
4 cloves garlic, minced
8 oz brown or white mushrooms, roughly sliced
1 1/2 tsp dried thyme
1/2 tsp dried oregano
1 1/2 tsp turmeric (optional)
2 tbsp chopped fresh parsley, reserve half for garnish
1/4 tsp nutmeg
3 tbsp coconut flour
1/4 cup apple cider vinegar
4 cups chicken broth, plus extra (or water) to top up, as needed
1 cup whipping cream

Cream of chicken soup reminds me of skating on the pond, coming home freezing cold, and finding Mom waiting with a warm bowl of homemade chicken soup. Nothing hit the spot, warmed me up, and was gobbled up more than this soup.

I've adapted Mom's cream of chicken soup here—but I'm convinced she would love this version too.

This deeply flavoured soup can be served plain with just the broth or loaded with vegetables that build flavour. The vegetables can be blended into the broth with an immersion blender for added nutrients and goodness.

1. Season the chicken cubes with salt and pepper.
2. Place the oil in a large Dutch oven or stockpot and heat on a medium heat. Place the chicken cubes in the hot oil and cook until the outside edges turn golden, about 2 to 3 minutes. Do not overfill the bottom of the pan. Work in small batches.
3. Remove the chicken to a bowl when it is fully cooked. For a chunky soup, separate half the chicken and mince it finely with a knife. For a puréed, creamy soup, mince all the chicken. This will be added back into the broth before it is puréed.
4. In the same pot, pour the oil directly into the chicken juices on a medium heat. Add the onion, carrots, and celery. Cook, stirring occasionally, until tender, about 5 to 7 minutes. Stir in the mushrooms, garlic, and spices and cook for about 3 minutes or until the vegetables are mostly cooked through. Check the seasoning and adjust the salt and pepper if needed.
5. For a puréed soup, remove the vegetables now to a bowl. For a chunky version of this soup, leave the vegetables in.
6. Sprinkle the flour in the pan and whisk it into the juices. Cook until lightly browned, about 1 to 3 minutes.
7. Deglaze the pan with the vinegar. Add it to the pan and turn the heat to high, stirring it into the flour mixture. Cook for about 5 minutes. Whisk in the chicken stock, and cook, whisking constantly, until slightly thickened, about 7 to 8 minutes. Reduce the heat. Simmer for about 20 minutes to allow the flavours to come together and the desired thickness is reached. Stir in the whipping cream until it is heated through, but do not boil. Check the seasoning and adjust with salt and pepper to taste.
8. Return the minced chicken to the pot and let it cool slightly. Purée with an immersion blender or pour the cooled soup into a blender.
9. Check the seasoning and adjust with salt and pepper to taste.
10. Spoon into a shallow bowl and spoon a generous portion of the chicken and vegetables directly into the middle of the bowl.
11. Garnish with a sprinkle of parsley and chicken scratchins (see page 70).

▶ OPTIONAL: CHICKEN SCRATCHINS

1. Preheat the oven to 275°F and line a baking sheet with parchment paper.
2. Scrape the excess fat from the skins and season with salt, pepper, garlic, and thyme.
3. Spread the skins on the prepared baking sheet and cover with another sheet of parchment paper. Place another baking sheet on top of the parchment paper and place it in the oven. Roast for 10 to 15 minutes and then check the skins.
4. Rotate the baking sheet and roast for 10 or 15 minutes more or until the skins are cooked through.

NOTE: Omit the turmeric for a whiter soup. The vinegar acts as a flavour enhancer and it cooks off and mellows as the soup simmers. Scratchins should be cooked through with the fat/skin fully rendered. If the skins are not fully rendered, they will not crisp fully. Skins will crisp as they cool.

SOUPS AND STEWS | 71

Fennel Soup

2 tbsp butter or oil
1 medium onion, diced
2 medium fennel bulbs, cut in small pieces, green tops chopped, fronds reserved for garnish
1 garlic clove, minced
1 carrot, shredded or ribboned with a carrot peeler
1 tsp fennel seeds, crushed or pulverized
1 tsp salt
1/2 tsp pepper
1/2 tsp dried thyme
1/2 tsp ground coriander
6 cups chicken or vegetable broth
1/2 cup whipping cream

Most people describe fennel as having an anise or licorice flavour. That made me very hesitant to try it—even the smell of licorice candy does me in.

When I finally gave fennel a go, I was pleasantly surprised. The flavour of uncooked fennel is fresh, delicate, and mild and not at all like licorice. When it is cooked, it has a subtle almost nutty, sweet taste.

1. Place the butter in a large saucepan on a medium-high heat. Add the onion and fennel and cook until the onion softens, about 3 minutes. Add the garlic and spices and cook for about 3 minutes more, stirring constantly. Add the broth and bring to a boil, then reduce the heat to a simmer. Cook until the fennel is tender, about 15 minutes. Remove from the heat and allow it to slightly cool.
2. Purée the soup with an immersion blender or food processor. Return the puréed soup to the stockpot on a low heat and stir in the cream. Check the seasoning and adjust to taste.
3. Serve with a drizzle of good-quality oil and a sprinkle of the fennel fronds.

NOTE: Add 1/2 to 1 teaspoon (to taste) of Korean chili flakes to increase the spiciness. For a heartier soup, add 1 medium celeriac diced in 1/2-inch squares with the fennel and onion. Do not let the contents of the pot boil after the cream has been added, as this can cause the soup to split. This soup freezes well. If freezing, do not add the cream until after it has thawed.

Italian Wedding Soup

FOR THE MEATBALLS

1 tsp ground cumin
1 tsp dried parsley
1 tsp dried oregano
1 tsp fennel seeds, crushed
1 tsp salt
1/2 tsp pepper
1/2 tsp dried thyme
1/2 tsp dried basil
1/2 tsp pepper
1/4 tsp dried rosemary
2 tbsp yellow (or Dijon) mustard
3 oz grated Parmesan cheese
1 large egg
3 cloves garlic, minced
1 medium onion, diced
1 1/2 lb ground pork

FOR THE SOUP

2 tbsp oil
1 medium onion, roughly chopped
3 cloves garlic, minced
1 medium carrot, diced
1 lb celeriac, diced
2 sticks celery, diced
6-8 cups chicken broth
1 cup fresh spinach, chard,
   or other greens, coarsely chopped
2 large eggs
1 oz grated Parmesan cheese,
   plus more for garnish
1/4 tsp nutmeg
1 tsp salt and 1/2 tsp pepper, or to taste

chopped fresh parsley, for garnish

Back in the day, Geoff and I ate at Italian restaurants a fair bit. Italian Wedding Soup was my favourite go-to for lunch: a hearty meatball soup with Italian flavours. It always hit the spot perfectly.

Make double batches of meatballs and freeze them for a quick and easy pot of soup for weeknights.

To prepare the meatballs
1. Combine the spices with the mustard, cheese, and egg. Mix well. Add the garlic, onion, and pork.
2. With a very light hand, mix all the ingredients together. The more you handle the mixture, the tougher the meatballs will be. Carefully form into balls about 1 inch in diameter. Bake at 350°F for 20 to 25 minutes. Remove from the oven and set aside.

To prepare the soup
1. Pour the oil into a large stockpot on a medium-high heat. When the oil is hot, add the onion and sauté until it turns translucent. Add the garlic and continue to cook for another 2 to 3 minutes. Add the celeriac, carrot, and celery and cook until tender, about 10 to 15 minutes, depending on the size of the vegetables. Add the chicken broth and bring to a boil, then reduce the heat to a simmer. Add the greens and cook until soft. Check the seasoning and adjust.
2. Turn off the heat. Meanwhile, in a separate bowl, whisk the eggs and cheese together. Stirring the soup in one direction, drizzle in the egg mixture to form thin ribbons of egg.
3. Place the meatballs in each bowl.
4. Ladle the soup into the bowls and top with cheese and parsley.

NOTE: For a tomatoey variation, add 1 can chopped tomatoes, as well as an extra 1 teaspoon dried oregano, 1 teaspoon dried parsley, and 1/2 teaspoon dried basil. Meatballs may be cooked on a medium-low heat on the stovetop instead of in the oven. For a pasta element in the soup, add konjac/shirataki alfredo noodles that have been cut in 1-inch pieces.

Jalapeño Popper Soup

2 tbsp oil
2 boneless, skinless chicken breasts
1/2 lb bacon, chopped in 1/2-inch pieces
1 medium onion, minced
4 jalapeño peppers, minced
1/2 bell pepper, chopped
2 cloves garlic, minced
1 tsp ground cumin
1 tsp chili powder
1 tsp salt
1/2 tsp pepper
1/4 cup apple cider vinegar
4 cups chicken broth
4 oz cream cheese, at room temperature
2 cups whipping cream, at room temperature

Optional garnish
grated cheddar, Monterey Jack, or any sharp cheese
sautéed jalapeño slices
sour cream
chopped green onion or chives

The shredded chicken adds a rustic element to this spicy soup. It can be cut in thin slices or cubes, but we recommend letting your rustica casa (rustic home) style show.

Remove all seeds and ribs from the jalapeño to reduce the spiciness. Add a few dashes of hot sauce for extra heat.

1. Place the oil in a large stockpot on a medium-high heat. Sauté the chicken breasts, bacon, and onion until the chicken is cooked through. Remove the chicken and set aside. Deglaze the pan with water. Add the jalapeños, green pepper, garlic, and spices and sauté for about 5 minutes, until the peppers and garlic soften. Deglaze with the vinegar. Add the broth and continue to simmer for 30 minutes.
2. Turn off the heat and mix in the cream cheese and cream. Whisk to incorporate. Check the seasoning and adjust to taste.
3. Shred the chicken breasts and place a generous portion in the bottom of each bowl.
4. Spoon the broth over the chicken and add the desired garnish.

Portuguese Fish Stew

FOR THE FISH

1 1/2 lb cod or halibut, cut in 2-inch cubes
2 tbsp lime juice
1/2 tsp salt
1/4 tsp pepper

FOR THE BROTH

2 tbsp oil
1 medium onion, diced
1 tsp salt
1/2 tsp pepper
1 red bell pepper, roughly sliced
1 tbsp ground cumin
1 tbsp paprika
1/2 tsp ground cardamom
1/4 tsp nutmeg
1/4 tsp ground ancho chili, or 1 tsp chili powder
5 cloves garlic, minced
1 14-oz can tomatoes, diced
1 cup vegetable, chicken, or fish broth
3/4 cup canned coconut milk
6-8 large shrimp, peeled, and deveined with tails intact

TO FINISH

1 bunch of fresh parsley or cilantro
drizzle of oil

This is a gorgeous fish stew that we fell in love with while celebrating our wedding anniversary at a Caribbean resort. Most of the food offered on the menu was heavy on the meat side, but this stew was full of rich broth, fish, and veggies.

This stew, known as *Caldeirada de Peixe*, is a fresh medley of fish and vegetables, slowly cooked in a tomato broth. This hodgepodge originated with the fishers themselves. It was a quick and easy supper, using whatever fish and greens were in season and abundant. Perhaps this is why every region of Portugal has its own variation of this rustic stew.

I'm willing to bet no matter what fish or spice combination is used, the result is heartwarming and satisfying.

To prepare the fish
1. Place the cod, lime juice, garlic, salt, and pepper in a glass bowl and stir well to incorporate. Set aside to marinate while preparing the broth.

To prepare the broth
1. Heat the oil in a large cast-iron pot or Dutch oven on a medium heat. Add the onion, salt, and pepper and sauté until the onion is translucent, about 3 minutes. Add the bell pepper with the onion and cook for 3 minutes more. Stir in the spices, garlic, and tomato paste. Let the paste bloom and cook for about 1 minute; add the tomatoes and chicken broth and continue to cook for 2 to 3 minutes. Use a wooden spoon to ensure that all the brown bits are scraped from the bottom of the pan into the broth.
2. Reduce the heat and stir in the coconut milk. Simmer on a low heat, stirring occasionally, until the sauce thickens, about 3 to 4 minutes.
3. Tuck the shrimp and cod pieces into the broth and cover. Cook for 3 for 4 minutes or until the cod is just cooked through. Check the seasoning and adjust the salt or pepper if needed. Stir in the chopped parsley or cilantro just before serving.
4. Spoon the stew into bowls and drizzle a little oil into each bowl to finish.

NOTE: Do not marinate the cod for more than 30 minutes.

Roasted Green Tomato Soup

FOR THE FINISHING OIL
1/2 cup fresh parsley
1/2 cup fresh basil
1/4 tsp salt
1/2 cup olive oil

FOR THE SOUP
2 lb green tomatoes, roughly chopped
1 medium onion, roughly chopped
4-6 garlic cloves, whole
2 tbsp oil
2 tsp salt
1 tsp pepper
1 tbsp butter
1/4 tsp Korean chili flakes
4 cups chicken or vegetable stock
1/4 cup apple cider vinegar
1/4 cup fresh basil, minced
1/4 cup fresh parsley, minced
1/8 cup fresh thyme leaves
1/3 tsp dried tarragon
4 slices cooked bacon, crumbled
1 tsp powdered sweetener
pinch of nutmeg

TO FINISH
4 slices cooked bacon, crumbled
drizzle of whipping cream
finishing oil

A rich and aromatic soup that is perfect for a fall day after harvest.

The flavour of this sophisticated younger sibling to a traditional tomato soup is robust and bright. Its unmistakable sour zing is only found in new green tomatoes.

Make the finishing oil first so the flavours and colours of the ingredients have time to marry. The oil not only completes the look but also adds an herb-alicious pop of flavour.

Use an immersion blender to purée this soup, or purée the vegetables in a food processor before adding the liquid and spices.

To prepare the finishing oil
1. Combine all the ingredients in a glass bowl and stir well. Set aside and stir often. Allow time for the colour and flavour to bloom.

To prepare the soup
1. Preheat the oven to 400°F.
2. Place the tomatoes, onion, and garlic on a baking sheet lined with parchment paper and drizzle with the oil. Sprinkle salt and pepper on the vegetables and toss to evenly coat. Roast for about 45 minutes to 1 hour, until soft and starting to colour. Transfer the vegetables to a food processor and purée.
3. Place the purée in a large stockpot. Add the remaining ingredients, except the garnish, and bring to a boil. Reduce the heat to a simmer and cook for 20 to 25 minutes. Add extra water or broth as needed.
4. Serve with a drizzle of cream, finishing oil, and a sprinkle of crumbled bacon.

Stinging Nettle Soup
➤ EXTRA: STINGING NETTLE PESTO

2 tbsp oil
1 medium onion, diced
1 cup celeriac, jicama, or daikon,
   cut in 1/2-inch cubes
1 carrot, ribboned with a carrot peeler
3 cloves garlic, minced
2 tsp fresh tarragon,
   or 1 tsp dried tarragon
1 tsp salt
1 tsp dried thyme
1/2 tsp pepper
1/4 tsp nutmeg
4 cups vegetable or chicken stock
6 cups young/tender stinging nettle
   leaves, leaves only (wear gloves
   to handle stinging nettles),
   or baby spinach leaves
1/4 cup apple cider vinegar

sour cream or whipping cream, for garnish
fresh chives or parsley, for garnish

FOR THE STINGING NETTLE PESTO

2 cups stinging nettle leaves, with stems
   removed (wear gloves)
1/2 cup olive oil
3-4 large garlic cloves, minced
2 oz grated Parmesan cheese
1/4 cup pine nuts, almonds, or pistachios
1 tbsp lemon juice
1/2 tsp salt
1/4 tsp pepper

Why would anyone want to eat a bowl of stinger soup?

Not only are stinging nettles edible (leaves, stems, and roots), this nutritional powerhouse is full of vitamins and protein, as well as being delicious and free. Stinging nettles have a long history of use as a medicinal herb, for kidney function (it is even believed to help dissolve kidney stones) and for lowering blood glucose levels.

The sting comes from formic acid (which causes irritation, redness, swelling, and pain) in the tiny hairs that cover the plant. These hairs lose their ability to sting when they are cooked or dehydrated.

1. Place the oil in a medium stockpot on a medium-high heat. Sauté the onion and celeriac for 5 to 7 minutes until the onion starts to turn translucent. Add the garlic and carrot and cook for another 2 to 3 minutes before adding the spices.
2. Deglaze the pan by adding the vinegar. Use a spatula or wooden spoon to ensure that all the brown bits have been scraped off the bottom of the pan.
3. Add the broth and, using gloves or tongs, carefully add the stinging nettles and reduce the heat to low. Stir to ensure that the stinging nettles are submerged and simmer to wilt them. Simmer for about 10 minutes. Do not boil. Turn off the heat and let the pot cool.
4. Once the soup has cooled, blend with an immersion blender until very smooth. Adjust the seasoning and add extra salt and pepper if needed.
5. Spoon into bowls and top with a swirl of whipping or sour cream.
6. Sprinkle with fresh chives or a sprig of parsley.

➤ STINGING NETTLE PESTO

1. Boil the stinging nettle leaves for at least 5 minutes. Strain (reserve the water) and transfer to a blender with the remaining ingredients and pulse. Add more olive oil if necessary.
2. The pesto is done when it reaches the consistency of a thick spreadable paste or sauce.
3. Serve on steak, pork, chicken, or fish, spread it on roasted vegetables, or use it as a pizza sauce.

NOTE: Reserve the vitamin-rich cooking water for tea or to water plants. Harvest immature stinging nettle plants that are less than 1 foot tall. Mature leaves are bitter and may contain cystoliths (a mineral deposit that often causes bladder or kidney stones), which can cause kidney irritation. When stinging nettles are not in season, use spinach or any other rich/deep green. If stung by stinging nettles, wait 10 minutes and then wash the area with soap and cool water. Use sticky tape to remove any remaining fibres. Antihistamines and/or a cold compress alleviates the itching/irritation and pain. Freeze extra pesto in ice cube trays.

Taco Soup

2 tbsp oil
1 medium yellow onion, diced
1 lb ground beef, minced pork, or precooked shredded chicken
1 green bell pepper, diced, or equivalent jalapeño peppers for extra heat
5 cloves garlic, minced
2 tbsp chili powder
1 tsp ground cumin
1 tsp ground coriander
1 tsp paprika
1 tsp Korean chili flakes
2 tsp sea salt
2 tsp dried oregano
1 28-oz can tomatoes, undrained
4 cups chicken or vegetable broth
2 cups water
1 cup sliced black olives
1/2 cup canned chopped green chilies

TOPPINGS
grated old cheddar, Monterey Jack, or any sharp cheese
chopped green or red onions
diced avocado
crumbled pork rinds
sour cream
sliced jalapeño peppers

Everybody loves a cup of warm soup on a cold day and this taco soup is doubly that; it is not only temperature warm but also warm from its blend of spices. The secret is in the balance and blend of the spices: spiced but not spicy.

Have a bowl just as it is or pile it high with optional toppings.

1. Place the oil, onion, and beef/pork (if using chicken, add last) in a large stockpot on a medium-high heat.
2. Cook, while breaking apart the meat, until the onions turn translucent.
3. Add the peppers, garlic, and spices, and cook for 3 minutes.
4. Add the remaining ingredients (except chicken) and adjust the seasoning. Reduce the heat to low and simmer 15 to 20 minutes.
5. Add chicken (if using), stir, cover, and let it sit for 5 minutes before serving.

NOTE: Stir 2 to 4 ounces cream cheese into the broth to reduce the heat.

White Asparagus (Spargel) Soup

❖ **VARIATION: BBQ IN A BOWL**

2 tbsp butter or oil
1/2 cup onion, chopped
2 cloves garlic, minced
1 lb white asparagus, peeled and cut in 1-inch pieces, heads reserved
6 cups chicken or vegetable broth
2 tsp salt
1 tsp pepper, white preferred
1/2 cup whipping cream
2 large egg yolks
1/4 cup dry white wine or apple cider vinegar

fresh parsley or chives, chopped, for garnish

This one is Geoff's story to tell ...

Thirty years ago I was working with the Department of National Defense at CFB Baden in Germany and decided to take a tour around the area. We were driving on the outskirts of a small town in the German countryside, an area locally referred to as spargel dorf (asparagus village), near where the white asparagus grew in the Black Forest.

Everywhere we looked were rows upon rows of unusual white mounds. When we stopped to refuel, a local resident explained that as the asparagus grew, the earth was mounded up around the young stems to prevent sunlight ever touching the stalks. The sunlight (and resulting chlorophyll) would turn the stalks green and completely change the taste of the tender stems.

Of course, we had to sample the local soup before we moved on. It reminded me of a creamed corn soup, a flavour that I thoroughly enjoyed.

You can make this soup with green asparagus, but if you can get your hands on the white variety, grab it fast and make spargel soup.

1. Place the butter in a large stockpot on a medium heat. Add the onion and sauté until it softens and turns translucent, about 3 minutes. Add the garlic and cook for another 2 minutes. Do not let the onion and garlic brown, as this is a white soup. Add the asparagus and broth, bring to a boil, then reduce the heat and simmer until the asparagus is tender, about 20 minutes.
2. Allow to cool for about 10 minutes, then purée the soup with an immersion blender.
3. Mix the whipping cream and egg yolks in a small bowl. With the heat still off, very slowly drizzle or stir the egg mixture into the soup and continue to stir gently for a few minutes until the egg yolks have thickened the soup.
4. Return the soup to a low heat. Bring the soup to a simmer and add the reserved asparagus tips. Cook gently for about 5 minutes until they are cooked through. Garnish with a drizzle of oil and a sprinkle of parsley or chives.

NOTE: If the asparagus is woody, the soup may need to be strained through a fine sieve. Xanthan gum may be added into the soup to thicken it.

❖ VARIATION: BBQ IN A BOWL

This is our take on a corn velouté that is dressed up for a BBQ. That traditional creamy corn soup (a velouté is a soup thickened with flour) is high in carbs. Our version tastes like corn but it contains none. To the basic soup recipe above add:
1 tsp fresh parsley
1/4 cup nutritional yeast

To garnish the bowl
pieces of precooked faux-tatoes, such as daikon or celeriac
pieces of beef, precooked and coated in BBQ sauce (page 171)
drizzle of oil
chopped fresh parsley or chives

To plate
1. Place the warm faux-tatoes in a pile in the centre of a bowl and gently pour the soup into the bottom of the bowl, taking care not to topple the faux-tatoes.
2. Place the BBQ meat on the faux-tatoes. Garnish with a drizzle of oil and a sprinkle of parsley or chives before serving.

SOUPS AND STEWS | 89

Veggie Dishes and Sides

It's Not Easy Being Green...

Avocado and Tomato Salad
Best Faux-Tato Salad
Braised Baby Bok Choy
Eggplant Lasagna
Faux Mac and Cheese
Faux Tater Tots
Fennel Slaw
Irish Colcannon
Oven Roasted Veg
Ratatouille—Imam Bayildi
Ravioli with Brown Butter Sauce
Roasted Carrots with Carrot Top Chimichurri
Skeddi Ohs
Sunday Roast Confit Faux-Tatoes
Veggie Curry—Nine Gem Korma
Whole Roasted Cauliflower

What's the deal with veggies? Why do they have so many carbs? Are there good carbs and bad carbs? Shouldn't it be everything in moderation?

These are questions that I hear often in coaching sessions. The answers are not so simple. We will get most of our carbs from veggies, but while nobody ever got fat eating a piece of broccoli, it's a good idea to know which vegetables should be limited and why.

Green and/or leafies are your friend. I wouldn't consider them or any food a free for all but it's fine to have a normal-sized portion of these.

The white replacements offered in this section, faux versions of pasta, rice, and potatoes, should have dialed-back serving sizes. It's important to learn to recompose our plate: gone is the bed of any of these foods; instead, use these foods as a small side serving and an every-once-in-a-while add-on, not an everyday staple.

It's a matter of changing our mindset and our habits, not just the individual components of what we eat. Eating a slice of bread every day before we got healthy wasn't good for us and eating the faux versions every day is not a good thing now. Don't fall into the habit of needing faux/replacements every day.

Moderation works when it's items that our bodies were meant to process. Taking our diets back to simple ingredients and away from processed and ultra-refined foods is a good thing. The more we move toward more natural foods the more we move toward dietary freedom.

Dial back the white replacements and lean into those green—and you'll find the road to health and being green isn't that hard after all.

Avocado and Tomato Salad

❖ **VARIATION: STRAWBERRY SPINACH SALAD**

FOR THE SALAD
1 ripe avocado
juice of 1 lime
1 cup halved cherry tomatoes
2 oz crumbled feta cheese
1/4 cup thinly sliced red onion
1/4 cup roughly chopped fresh parsley

FOR THE DRESSING
2 tbsp powdered sweetener
1/2 cup olive oil
1/8 cup white balsamic vinegar
1 tsp salt
1 tbsp Dijon mustard
1 tsp onion, minced
1 tsp poppy seeds
2 cloves garlic, minced
1 tsp salt
1/2 tsp pepper
1/2 tsp dried thyme
1/4 tsp Korean chili flakes
   or alternate heat

This salad is easy to customize. Pare it down to just tomato, feta, onions, and dressing, or dress it up with strawberries, spinach, and pecans. It is light, refreshing, super versatile, and can be paired with many meals.

To prepare the salad
Halve the avocados, remove the pits, and dice. Squeeze fresh lime juice over them and gently toss to coat with the juice. Place all the ingredients in a serving bowl.

To prepare the dressing
Place all the ingredients in a Mason jar and shake vigorously to combine. Pour over the salad and toss at the table.

NOTE: To emulsify the dressing, add 1/8 teaspoon sunflower lecithin.

❖ **VARIATION: STRAWBERRY SPINACH SALAD**
Substitute the feta cheese with an equal amount of goat cheese and add 1/2 cup chopped strawberries, 1/4 cup pecans, and 1 1/2 cups baby spinach for a gorgeous summer salad.

Best Faux-Tato Salad

FOR THE SALAD

1 large celeriac, peeled, roughly chopped in 1/2-inch cubes, precooked

1 tsp salt

1/2 tsp pepper

6-8 cherry tomatoes, diced

2 tsp minced chives

2 tbsp fresh parsley, or 1 tsp dried parsley

1/2 tsp fennel or dill fronds

FOR THE DRESSING

1/2 cup Mayonnaise (page 272)

1/4 cup apple cider vinegar

2 tbsp avocado or olive oil

1 tbsp Dijon mustard

2 tsp powdered sweetener, or to taste

2 tsp garlic powder

1 tsp onion powder

1 tsp paprika

1 tsp salt

1/2 tsp pepper

The full-octane version of this recipe was my go-to for any potlucks or backyard BBQs I attended in the past, so I knew it was one that I would tweak over to the healthy side someday.

As with all white replacements, easy does it on the serving size. This recipe is one that can get away from you (carb-wise) quite easily. Customize the flavour profile of this recipe with the seasoning profiles on page 166.

Bring this chunky rustic salad to the next backyard get-together.

To prepare the dressing
Put all the ingredients in a Mason jar and shake well or whisk together in a small bowl.

To prepare the salad
Mix all the ingredients in a medium mixing bowl. Stir the dressing through the salad and refrigerate. Serve cold.

NOTE: Even though these food choices are lower in carbs than traditional offerings, they should be consumed in moderation. Allow no more than 1/3 cup per meal.

Braised Baby Bok Choy

- 2 tbsp oil
- 2 baby bok choy, cut in half lengthways
- 1 tsp ground ginger, or 1/2 tsp grated fresh ginger
- 1/2 tsp garlic powder
- 1/2 cup water
- 1/2 tsp salt
- 1/4 tsp pepper
- 1/2 tsp Korean chili flakes or paprika (optional)

This delicately spiced and tender side of vegetables will accompany most meat dishes, especially a steak or a piece of white fish.

Bok choy, which translates from Cantonese to "white vegetable," has a slightly bitter taste similar to other dark leafy members of the brassica (cabbage) family. Baby bok choy is a sweet, mild-tasting immature version of the adult plant.

Geoff likes his baby bok choy spicy, so he adds Korean chili flakes, while I prefer the cleaner taste of the veggies with ginger. Use the seasoning profiles on page 166 and make this a different dish every time.

1. Season the cut side of the bok choy with salt and pepper.
2. Place the oil in a large sauté pan on a medium-high heat. When the pan is hot, add the halved bok choy cut side down and cook for 3 to 4 minutes or until the face of the bok choy is slightly caramelized and turning brown. Season the top side of the bok choy with salt and pepper while the cut side is cooking. Flip the bok choy to cut side up and add Korean chili flakes (if using). Add the ginger, garlic, and water.
3. Cover and steam until the bok choy is tender and the liquid has been cooked off, about 3 to 5 minutes.
4. Remove from the pan and serve.

Eggplant Lasagna WITH BÉCHAMEL

FOR THE ROASTED TOMATO SAUCE

6-8 vine-ripened tomatoes, quartered
1/8-1/4 cup olive oil
1 tsp salt
1/2 tsp pepper
2 tbsp oil
1 shallot, finely diced
4 cloves garlic, peeled and minced
1 tbsp finely chopped fresh oregano
1 tsp chopped fresh marjoram,
    or 1/2 tsp dried marjoram

FOR THE ROASTED PEPPERS

3 red bell peppers, quartered and seeded
2 tbsp olive oil
1 tsp dried parsley
1/2 tsp dried thyme
salt and pepper, to taste

FOR THE BÉCHAMEL SAUCE

1 tbsp butter
1 tbsp coconut flour
1/2 tsp pepper
1/2 cup whipping cream
4-6 oz grated Parmesan cheese
1/4 cup ricotta cheese
1 large egg, lightly beaten

I'm not a vegetarian, but I enjoy many vegetarian dishes.

When they're done right, they are a comfort meal unto themselves and need nothing extra to complete or complement them. That is the case with this eggplant lasagna.

This lasagna is layered upside down in the pan and flipped, so the first layer you put in the bottom of the pan, when flipped, will become the top presentation layer. We use a combination of wraps and eggplant to serve as the lasagna sheets. Add the béchamel sauce and top it all off with roasted tomato sauce for a knockout meal.

To prepare the roasted tomato sauce
1. Preheat the oven to 350°F and line a baking sheet with parchment paper.
2. Place the quartered tomatoes skin side down on the prepared sheet, drizzle with oil, and season with spices. Roast for 1 to 1 1/2 hours or until slightly dehydrated. Set aside to cool.
3. When the tomatoes are cooled, roughly chop them.
4. Place the oil in a large sauté pan on a medium heat. When the oil is hot, add the shallot and garlic, and cook for about 3 minutes. Add the tomatoes and check the seasoning. Simmer until the sauce thickens to the desired consistency. This should be a thick rustic sauce.

To prepare the roasted peppers
1. Reset the oven to 400°F and line a baking sheet with parchment paper.
2. Place the peppers cut side down on the prepared sheet and roast for 20 to 30 minutes or until the skin blisters. Transfer the roasted peppers to a bowl and cover tightly with plastic wrap. After 10 minutes, peel and discard the skins. Set aside.

To prepare the béchamel sauce
1. Melt the butter in a medium sauté pan, stir in the flour and pepper, and cook for 1 minute.
2. Whisk in the whipping cream and cook until slightly thickened. Remove from the heat, and cool slightly.
3. Add the Parmesan and ricotta cheeses and egg and stir to combine. Check seasoning, cover, and set aside.

VEGGIE DISHES AND SIDES | 99

TO ASSEMBLE

1 medium eggplant, cut lengthwise in 1/2-inch-thick slices

1 tsp salt

olive oil

3-4 green zucchini, cut lengthwise in 1/2-inch-thick slices

roasted peppers (recipe above)

soft tortilla wraps (page 141)

béchamel sauce (recipe above)

fresh spinach (optional)

To assemble

1. Brush both sides of the eggplant with oil and sear in a hot sauté pan for 1 to 2 minutes until golden. Set aside. Repeat this process with the zucchini.
2. Grease mini loaf or small lasagna pans with Baker's Magic (Pan) Release (page 273) and line the bottom and sides with parchment paper, leaving at least 1 inch sticking up over the sides.
3. Preheat the oven to 350°F.
4. Begin with a layer of eggplant cut to fit the bottom of the pan, followed by a wrap.
5. Next a thin layer of béchamel, roasted pepper, and roasted zucchini, and then a layer of spinach (if using).
6. Repeat these layers, ending with a layer of zucchini. When the lasagna is flipped, this final layer will become the bottom of the lasagna.
7. Cover the lasagna with a sheet of parchment paper cut to size and laid directly on the zucchini, and then cover the pan with aluminum foil.
8. Bake for 25 to 30 minutes until a fork pierces the lasagna easily and all the layers are soft.

NOTE: Use mini loaf pans for individual servings or make this into a family-size casserole. Use a mandoline to make uniformly thin slices.

Faux Mac and Cheese

4 tbsp butter

2 tbsp coconut flour

1/2 cup whipping cream

10 oz grated old cheddar, Swiss, or Gruyère cheese, or any combination of cheeses

1 oz grated Parmesan cheese

3 oz cream cheese

1 tsp garlic powder

1/2 tsp paprika

1/4 cup broth

1/4 tsp pepper

2 14-oz (400 g) cans hearts of palm, half moons

4 oz grated mild cheese (mozzarella or Gruyère), for topping

1 cup crushed pork rinds

2 tbsp butter, at room temperature

1/2 tsp pepper

Hearts of palm stalks were a normal ingredient to find in our kitchen for Skeddi Ohs (page 122) and as lasagna. When we found the half-moon version of this pasta replacement, we immediately thought of mac and cheese and our faux mac and cheese recipe was created.

This recipe makes enough sauce for triple the faux mac recipe! Batch-cook the sauce and freeze it in freezer bags, or increase the number of hearts of palm and make a bigger batch of faux mac and cheese for the freezer.

Pair with a chicken breast and a serving of broccoli.

1. In a medium sauté pan, melt the butter on a medium heat. Whisk in the coconut flour until fully combined. Whisk in the whipping cream and cook for about 2 minutes. Add all the other ingredients. Allow the cheese mixture to come to a boil, then reduce the heat to a simmer. Simmer for 8 to 10 minutes or until the cheesy mixture coats the back of a spoon. Set aside.
2. Preheat the oven to 375°F and grease a casserole dish.
3. Boil the hearts of palm for 15 to 20 minutes or until the pieces are fork-tender. While this is boiling, combine the crust ingredients in a medium mixing bowl.
4. Drain the hearts of palm, rinse, and pat dry.
5. Combine the hearts of palm with the cheese sauce in a casserole dish. Sprinkle the grated cheese on the top and then the crispy coating. Bake for 20 minutes covered, then remove the cover. Cook uncovered for about 12 to 15 minutes or until the top is slightly browned and bubbly.

NOTE: If half-moon-shaped hearts of palm are hard to find, buy the (canned) full stalks and cut them in 1/4-inch discs and then cut each disc in half. Substitute almond flour for the pork rinds, if needed. No salt is added to this dish, as the cheeses make it salty enough.

Faux Tater Tots

❖ **VARIATION: HERBED SPINACH TOTS**

2 cups celeriac, precooked, drained well, and minced
1/4 cup coconut flour
2 oz grated old, white cheddar cheese
2 oz grated Parmesan cheese
1 large egg
2 tbsp nutritional yeast
1 tbsp onion powder
1 tsp garlic powder
1 tsp dried parsley (optional)
1/2 tsp pepper
1 large egg
1/4 cup water
1 cup crushed pork rinds or almond flour
1/2 tsp salt
1/2 tsp garlic powder
1/4 tsp pepper

These are our version of the frozen tater tots from the grocery store that we all know and love. They're crispy, crunchy, and fun.

In the culinary world, these would be known as croquettes, a small ball or roll of (usually) mashed potato or meat rolled in crumbs and fried, resulting in a soft centre and a crispy crunchy crust. The word *croquette* has French roots from croquer, which means to crunch or to bite.

If you're really crafty, you can make these look like the tater tots you buy in the shop. The kids will never know, and the adults will love them too.

1. Line a baking sheet with parchment paper.
2. Mix all the ingredients and form into 1- by 1/2-inch parcels and place on the prepared sheet.
3. Mix the egg and water in a small mixing bowl. Set aside.
4. Mix all the dredge ingredients in a flat-bottomed shallow dish such as a pie plate. Set in the refrigerator to chill for 20 minutes.
5. Carefully dip the chilled tots in the egg wash, then into the dredge ingredients, using a slotted spoon. Use a fork and spoon combination to fully cover the tots.
6. When all the tots are formed, refrigerate for 1 hour, or freeze for 30 minutes to set. Deep-fry in oil preheated to 350°F until golden, about 7 to 10 minutes.
7. Drain on a paper towel. Season and serve.

NOTE: The excess water must be drained out of the celeriac (or spinach) or the tots will not stick together when fried. The tots can be baked in a 400°F oven for 15 to 20 minutes instead of being deep-fried. If using this method, drizzle the tots with oil before placing them in the preheated oven.

❖ **VARIATION: HERBED SPINACH TOTS**

To the above recipe, add:

5 1/2 cups spinach, parboiled and drained well, chopped
4 oz cream cheese, at room temperature
1 cup fresh parsley or equivalent combined herbs, chopped
8 oz grated mozzarella cheese, to replace the cheeses above

Fennel Slaw

❖ **VARIATION: LEMON VINAIGRETTE**

FOR THE DRESSING
2/3 cup olive oil
1/3 cup white balsamic
    or apple cider vinegar
1/4 cup sour cream
2 garlic cloves, finely grated
    and then crushed to a paste
1 tsp salt
1/2 tsp poppy seeds or celery seed
1/4 tsp Korean chili flakes
squeeze of lemon juice
2 oz grated Parmesan cheese

FOR THE SALAD
2 fennel bulbs, thinly shaved
    on a mandoline, fronds reserved
1 medium onion, thinly shaved
    on a mandoline
1/4 cup thinly sliced white cabbage
3/4 cup of any of (or a combination of)
    fresh mint, basil, oregano, parsley,
    or tarragon, torn
fronds, for garnish

This bright and colourful salad works exceptionally well with grilled meats. The star of the dish is the fennel, but daikon, celeriac, or jicama can be substituted for the cabbage.

Combine all the dressing ingredients in a Mason jar and set aside. Assemble the slaw and toss with the slaw dressing. Garnish with fennel fronds and serve.

❖ **VARIATION: LEMON VINAIGRETTE**
Try this vinaigrette with orange instead of lemon (replace the juice and zest).
1 tsp lemon zest
1/4 cup lemon juice
2 tbsp apple cider vinegar
1/2 cup light tasting olive oil
2 cloves garlic, minced then
    pulverized to a paste
1 tsp salt
1/2 tsp pepper

VEGGIE DISHES AND SIDES | 107

Irish Colcannon

FOR THE CELERIAC

1/2 cup whipping cream
1 1/2 cups water
1 tsp salt
4 cloves garlic, quartered
1 large celeriac, about 1 lb peeled, cut in 1-inch cubes

FOR THE CABBAGE

3-4 cups thinly sliced Napa cabbage, spinach, or kale (ribs removed)
1 tsp salt

FOR THE CASSEROLE

4 oz butter
1/2 cup chopped fresh chives, thyme, or parsley
1 oz cream cheese
1/2 cup sour cream
1 tsp fresh parsley, for garnish
1 tsp salt
1/2 tsp pepper
4-5 green onions or scallions, sliced, for garnish

Our healthified version of Colcannon is even better than the real McCoy, or in an Irish sense better than the real O'Sullivan. Colcannon is a traditional Irish dish of mashed potatoes mixed with kale or cabbage. It is often served on Paddy's Day or at family get-togethers and Sunday dinners.

Our version uses celeriac mash as a potato replacement, and the faint taste of the celery root adds to the flavour.

1. Peel the celeriac, carefully digging out any cracks and crevices that could hide soil or dirt.
2. Bring the cream, water, and salt to a boil in a large saucepan on a medium-high heat. Add the celeriac cubes and garlic and bring to a boil. Reduce the heat to a low-medium heat and simmer for 20 minutes, or until the cubes are tender.
3. While the celeriac is boiling, place the cabbage and salt in another large pot of boiling water and boil until it has wilted, about 3 to 5 minutes. It should be slightly undercooked.
4. Drain the cabbage, then return it to the pot. Add one-third of the butter, cover, and set aside, off the heat.
5. Drain and place the celeriac cubes in a large mixing bowl.
6. Preheat the oven to 325°F.
7. Add one-third of the butter, cream cheese, sour cream, and spices and herbs to the celeriac and mash. As this is a chunky dish, it does not have to be perfectly smooth. Stir in the cabbage and adjust the seasoning.
8. Transfer the colcannon to an oven-safe baking dish and bake for 20 to 25 minutes covered.
9. Top with the remaining butter and sprinkle with the green onions.

NOTE: Because colcannon freezes and reheats well, this a great recipe to batch-cook.

Oven Roasted Veg

❖ **VARIATION: LEEKS AND FENNEL**

1 carrot, sliced in half lengthwise and then cut in diagonal slices
1/2 red onion, roughly chopped
1 cup broccoli, sliced in thick slabs
6-10 green beans
bacon fat, butter, or equivalent
1 tsp garlic powder
1/2 tsp Korean chili flakes
1/2 tsp dried thyme
salt and pepper, to taste

Sometimes all you need is veggies that are roasted up crispy and covered in healthy fats and spices. This is a great example of the term "brown means flavour." These veggies are all lovely steamed or boiled, but the browning adds so much to the taste.

Make this recipe your own by switching out the vegetables and spices for the ones your family will love.

1. Preheat the oven to 400°F and line a baking sheet with aluminum foil and parchment paper.
2. Working from the cutting board to the baking sheet, rub the vegetables with the bacon fat by hand and then sprinkle with the spices.
3. Do not add all the vegetables to the pan at once; add them according to their required cooking times. Beets, carrots, onion, and daikon need about 40 minutes; cauliflower, broccoli, cabbage, and garlic, about 25 minutes. Roast the vegetables, flipping the pieces midway, until golden brown, cooked through, and tender.

❖ **VARIATION: LEEKS AND FENNEL**
2 leeks or 2 fennel bulbs

For the fennel
Slice the fennel bulb in 1/4- to 1/3-inch pieces, keeping a portion of the stem intact to hold the fennel slice together. Use a mandoline for perfectly uniform pieces that will cook consistently. Continue with the instructions above.

For the leeks
1. With a sharp knife, remove the dark green leaf end, leaving what looks like a long onion. Keep about 2 to 3 inches of the light green part with the body of the leeks. Save the dark green parts for soups or a stew stock.
2. Slice the leek into slices about 1 to 1 1/2 inches thick and discard the root portion. Inspect the pieces of leek closest to the greens for dirt or debris. Rinse as needed. Stand them upright in an oven-safe pan and leave about 1/2 to 1 inch between each leek. Drizzle oil over the leeks and continue with the instructions above.

NOTE: If the leeks are soft and cooked through but not golden at the top, turn the oven to broil for 2 to 3 minutes (watch carefully) with the door slightly ajar.

Ratatouille – Imam Bayildi

➤ **EXTRA: PIPERADE VINAIGRETTE**

FOR THE PIPERADE SAUCE

1 tbsp oil
2 red bell peppers, diced
1 orange bell pepper, diced
1 28-oz can tomatoes, or 1 lb Roma or vine tomatoes with skins removed
1 medium onion, diced
4 cloves garlic, minced
1/2 cup red wine, or 1/4 cup broth and 1/4 cup vinegar
4 sprigs fresh thyme, or 1 tsp dry thyme
2 tbsp roughly chopped fresh basil, or 2 tsp dried basil
2 tbsp roughly chopped fresh parsley, or 2 tsp dried parsley
1 tsp salt
1/2 tsp pepper

FOR THE VEGGIE LAYERS

Slice all the vegetables in 1/8-inch-thick rounds:
- 2 Roma tomatoes
- 2-3 beets, or 1 yellow squash
- 1 zucchini
- 1 small onion or shallot
- 1 eggplant

If you've watched the movie *Ratatouille*, this dish will be familiar. Remy serves the cutthroat critic a snazzy version of this classic French Provençal "peasant dish." Pixar used Chef Thomas Keller as a food consultant to create the ratatouille, modelled after a Turkish dish called imam bayildi, which means "the imam fainted." Legend has it that it was so named after a Turkish priest who fainted with pleasure after his wife made him this meal.

Our sliced beet ratatouille is different from the traditional or movie version. The beet enhances and elevates the sauce. This ratatouille can be eaten warm or cold. It is best made in advance, the day before it is to be served. If using this option, fully cook then refrigerate for up to 3 days. Reheat the ratatouille covered in the oven and finish with the vinaigrette.

Reserve some piperade sauce to prepare the vinaigrette at the end: Remy used this sauce to make this dish epic and the critic's eyes pop.

Substitute yellow squash for the beet for a more traditional version.

To prepare the piperade sauce
1. Char the red pepper on the stovetop, BBQ, or gas grill until the whole skin is blackened. Remove from the heat, place directly in a glass bowl, and quickly cover the bowl with plastic wrap to allow the peppers to steam. Set aside for 10 minutes and then peel off the charred skin. A dry paper towel removes any stubborn pieces. Rinse with cool water. Remove the stem and seeds. Roughly chop and set aside.
2. Heat the oil in a large sauté pan on a medium heat. Add the onion and sauté until it turns translucent, about 3 to 4 minutes. Add the garlic and cook for 1 minute. Add the remaining ingredients except the red wine and cook for 5 to 8 minutes. Add the red wine. Stir to combine and simmer for 20 to 30 minutes or until the sauce has reduced and thickened. Remove from the heat and allow to cool.
3. Use a standard or immersion blender to purée the mixture.

To assemble
1. Preheat the oven to 375°F and grease a large oval (about 8-inch) baking dish.
2. Reserving 2 tablespoons sauce for the vinaigrette, pour the rest of the sauce into the dish. Arrange the vegetables, in an alternating pattern and overlapping so that 1/4 inch of each slice is exposed. Start at the edge and work toward the centre. Repeat until the entire pan is filled. Drizzle or brush a light layer of oil on the arranged vegetables. Finish with salt and pepper.
3. Cover and bake for 60 minutes, then uncover and bake for another 20 minutes or until the vegetables are tender. Drizzle with oil and the piperade vinaigrette (if using).
4. Serve immediately.

➤ **EXTRA: PIPERADE VINAIGRETTE**
This recipe can be done without the vinaigrette but we recommend trying it with this recipe extra at least once. To the reserved 2 tablespoons piperade sauce add:
2 tbsp olive oil
2 tsp white balsamic vinegar
2 tsp roughly chopped fresh herbs (thyme, parsley, basil, oregano)
1/2 tsp salt
1/4 tsp pepper
Shake in a Mason jar and drizzle over the finished ratatouille tableside.

NOTE: To oven-char the peppers, preheat the oven to 450°F. Place the pepper halves on an aluminum-foil-lined sheet cut side down. Roast until the skin loosens, about 20 to 25 minutes.

Ravioli WITH BROWN BUTTER SAUCE

FOR THE WRAPPERS

2 cups almond flour
1/3 cup coconut flour
3 tsp xanthan gum
1 tsp egg white powder
1/8 tsp salt
1 tbsp apple cider vinegar
1 large egg
1-3 tsp water

FOR THE FILLING

8 oz ricotta cheese
2 tbsp oil
2 cups baby spinach
2 cloves garlic
2 oz grated Parmesan cheese
1/8 cup pine nuts
1/2 tsp dried basil
1/4 tsp nutmeg
1/2 tsp salt
1 large egg yolk

FOR THE BROWN BUTTER SAUCE

1/2 cup butter
3 cloves garlic, minced
1 tbsp chopped fresh basil, sage, oregano, flat-leaf parsley, or chives and/or 1/2 tsp fresh thyme
1/2 tsp pepper
1 oz grated Pecorino, Romano, Asiago, or Parmesan cheese

Tomato or marinara sauce was all I knew when I was a kid. The thick tomato and (usually) cheesy sauces were all my immature palate needed to be satisfied.

Realizing that all pasta did not have to be served with a thick tomato sauce was an eye-opener, coming from a place where we always do it one way and learning brand new is sometimes a little daunting. This brown butter sauce with ravioli is a light and perfectly seasoned dish that will appeal to all ages.

The dough for this ravioli can be made using a food processor or by hand and the finished ravioli can be sautéed or boiled.

To prepare the filling
1. Place the oil in a sauté pan on a medium heat. Add the spinach and garlic and sauté until the spinach is totally wilted. Remove it from the pan and place it on a paper towel to cool off and absorb any excess liquid.
2. Use a knife or herb rocker to mince the spinach.
3. Combine all the filling ingredients. Mix well and set aside.

To prepare the wrappers with a food processor
1. Mix all the dry ingredients together in a food processor. Add the egg and vinegar, and gradually add the water in increments until a dough ball has formed. Remove the dough from the food processor and knead well by hand for about 5 minutes, then press into a ball.
2. Wrap the ball with plastic wrap and refrigerate it for 15 to 20 minutes.

To prepare the wrappers by hand
1. Mix all the dry ingredients together in a medium mixing bowl.
2. Add the egg and vinegar and then add the water in increments. The dough should be sticky and ready to form into a ball, with no cracks or crevices. Use a spatula to combine the ingredients. Knead the dough well by hand for about 5 minutes, then press into a ball. Wrap the ball with plastic wrap and refrigerate it for 15 to 20 minutes to chill.

To assemble
1. Roll out half of the ravioli dough between two sheets of parchment paper. The finished dough should be a large flat sheet that is almost translucent. Set aside. Repeat the process with the other half, trying to match the same basic shape as the first sheet.
2. Mound 1 to 1 1/2 teaspoons filling on the pasta, leaving 2 to 3 inches between each one.
3. Leaving the parchment paper intact, cover the filling with the second sheet of rolled-out dough. Remove the parchment paper and gently finger press the dough around the edges to remove all the excess air and then seal the edges around each ravioli piece.
4. Use a glass or ring to cut round pasta pieces, or cut them in squares. Gently brush water around the edge of the filling mixture to act as a seal.
5. Refrigerate the filled ravioli uncovered for 1 hour, or freeze for at least 20 minutes before cooking.

Sauté method
1. Place the butter and garlic in a medium saucepan on a medium heat.
2. When the butter has melted, add the ravioli (if you're not boiling) to the pan and cook on each side for 1 to 2 minutes.
3. Work in batches for the remaining ravioli, making sure that the garlic does not scorch. The butter should be a deep golden brown and not scorched.
4. Remove all ravioli and then remove the pan from the heat. Finish the brown butter sauce in the same pan by stirring in the herbs, pepper and cheese.

Boil method
1. Drop the ravioli into boiling, salted water and cook for about 6 to 7 minutes, depending on the size of the ravioli pieces. Remove them from the pot and drain well. Continue with the sauce directions above, cooking for 5 to 7 minutes or until the garlic butter is a deep golden brown.
2. Add the cooked ravioli to the sauce and stir through. Add the Parmesan cheese and garnish with more herbs to serve.

NOTE: If the garlic in the brown butter sauce is starting to brown too much, remove it from the pan and reserve it for garnish.

✔ **TIP**
Use any leftover filling to make stuffed chicken breasts.

Roasted Carrots
WITH CARROT TOP CHIMICHURRI

FOR THE CARROTS

3 cloves garlic, sliced
1 tbsp oil
1 tbsp Maple Syrup Substitute (page 283)
3 sprigs of fresh thyme, chopped
1 tsp salt
1/2 tsp pepper
1 lb carrots, washed, stems cut, leaving about 1 inch

FOR THE CHIMICHURRI

2 cups carrot tops, washed, dried, and finely chopped
1 cup fresh parsley and/or thyme
1/4 cup olive oil
1/2 tsp Korean chili flakes
3 cloves garlic, minced
1/2 tsp salt
1/2 tsp pepper
2 tbsp white balsamic vinegar
1 1/2 tbsp lemon juice

There's nothing like the taste of carrots, freshly pulled from your own garden—somehow, they are always a little sweeter when you grow them yourself.

It will be surprising to most people to learn that this vegetable can be eaten in its entirety: the tops are edible and delicious. Add them raw to green salads, or to soups and stews for added colour and flavour.

How better to dress these fresh veggies up for dinner than to use their own tops to make a chimichurri sauce? Chimichurri is most often made with parsley and garlic, but this version uses fresh carrot tops.

1. Mix all the chimichurri ingredients in a bowl. Set aside to allow the flavours to meld.
2. Preheat the oven to 400°F and line a baking sheet with aluminum foil and parchment paper. Set aside.
3. Place all the ingredients, except the carrots, in a large glass bowl. Mix thoroughly. Add the carrots and stir to combine, ensuring that the carrots are completely covered in the wet mixture. Transfer the carrots to the prepared baking sheet and put any of the remaining wet mixture on top of the carrots. Roast for 18 to 20 minutes, turning the carrots at the halfway mark. They should be soft throughout with the tips slightly charred when done. Remove from the oven and transfer to a serving plate. Set aside to cool.
4. Top with the chimichurri.

Did you know?
Save the carrot tops for use in the kitchen rather than discarding them. These edible tops are a source of vitamins C and K and are loaded with potassium. Use them in place of parsley or other herbs in recipes.

NOTE: This chimichurri freezes well. Freeze in an ice cream tray, then transfer the cubes to a freezer bag for individual portions that can be thawed easily.

Skeddi Ohs

2 tbsp oil
1 medium onion, diced
4 cloves garlic, minced
3-4 mushrooms, sliced
1 1/2 tsp dried oregano
1 tsp dried parsley
1/2 tsp dried thyme
1/2 tsp dried basil
1/2 tsp Korean chili flakes
1 12-oz can hearts of palm
1 1/2 cups tomato sauce
6-8 cherry tomatoes, halved
grated Parmesan cheese
3 or 4 fresh basil leaves, chiffonaded or thinly sliced (optional)

One of my favourite meals as a child was SpaghettiOs (we called them skeddi ohs) and toast. My grandparents had an old-fashioned general store and, whenever there, I had a full choice of the store shelves to choose my meals and snacks. My choice of meal was often cold Os and warm buttered toast. In my youth, I thought it was such a worldly, exotic thing to eat them cold from the can. It's a wonder I didn't have Os coming out of my ears, I ate it that often.

My tastes have changed as an adult and even more after starting on a journey of health. I no longer crave those empty fillers, now I want nutrient-dense food instead, but the kid in me still calls them skeddi ohs. This version provides the taste and comfort of that long-ago dish without a belly full of bloat.

To prepare the skeddi ohs

1. Mix all the ingredients in a bowl. Set aside to allow the flavours to meld. Heat the oil in a sauté pan on a medium heat and sauté the onion until translucent. Add the garlic and mushrooms and continue to cook for 3 minutes. Push the onion and garlic to the sides of the pan and add the herbs and spices, one by one, to the oil, then combine with the onions and garlic.
2. Add the hearts of palm and tomato sauce and reduce the heat to a simmer. Let simmer for at least 15 minutes.

To finish the dish

Add the tomatoes, just after the heat is turned off. Transfer to a plate and sprinkle with Parmesan cheese and fresh basil, if using.

NOTE: To make individual baked servings, dress ramekins/side plates with skeddi ohs and sauce and cover with cheese. Finish in a 350°F oven, or just long enough to melt the cheese and allow the sauce to marry with the skeddi ohs.

VEGGIE DISHES AND SIDES | 123

Sunday Roast Confit Faux-Tatoes

❖ **VARIATION: WEDGE FRIES**

1 celeriac, peeled, cleaned, and cut in 2-inch pieces
4-6 garlic cloves, peeled
1 tsp salt
1/2 tsp pepper
2 tsp chopped fresh thyme, oregano, and/or parsley
4 cups oil, or to cover (or 1 cup bacon fat and 3 cups olive oil)

A London Broil is similar to the traditional east coast family Sunday dinner, but the sides are baked or roasted and not boiled. Roasting these vegetables takes taste to a whole new level.

Our first London Broil was enjoyed in a lovely little pub just down the street from our hotel in London. Geoff's choice was lamb, while I opted for the roast beef version of this popular UK dish. But the real star of the dish was the roasted potatoes. They were just so different than what we were used to. We knew straight away that we would have to recreate and revise when we got home!

Finish in a deep fryer or oven-roast to crispy perfection.

1. Preheat the oven to 200°F.
2. The baking dish should hold the celeriac in a single layer, packed fairly tightly. Add all the ingredients and then cover completely with the oil. Bake for about 5 hours, checking frequently to ensure that all portions of the vegetables are covered by the oil. When cooked, remove the celeriac from the oil, and continue with one of the versions below.

Finishing technique 1
Preheat the oven to 400°F. Place the celeriac on a baking sheet with plenty of space between them to allow them to become crispy. Roast for about 30 to 40 minutes or until they are golden brown and crispy on the outside and very tender on the inside. Serve immediately, sprinkled with salt and pepper.

Finishing technique 2
Deep-fry the celeriac at 350°F until golden brown and crunchy on the outside. Toss in salt and pepper and serve.

❖ **VARIATION: WEDGE FRIES**
Dry the confit celeriac with a paper towel to remove all the oil and dip the individual pieces in an egg wash and then into the following spice combination.

1 cup almond flour
2 tsp garlic powder
1 1/2 tsp onion powder
1 tsp salt
1 tsp chili powder
1 tsp dried oregano
1/2 tsp smoked paprika
1/2 tsp pepper
1/2 tsp dried thyme

Continue with the baking instructions in finishing technique 1 above.

NOTE: I know it sounds like a very long time to cook a side dish, but once you get it all in the pot, you can go about your day and just check in every once in a while. The stove does the heavy lifting here.

Veggie Curry—Nine Gem Korma

FOR THE SPICE BLEND

2 tsp cumin seeds or 2 tsp ground cumin
2 tsp fennel seeds
1 tsp ground cardamom, or 4 cardamom pods
1 tsp whole black peppercorns
1/2 tsp cinnamon
5-6 garlic cloves
2 dried red chilies
1 tsp curry

FOR THE CURRY PASTE

2-inch piece of ginger, roughly chopped
5-6 cloves garlic, roughly chopped
2 large green chilies

FOR THE TEMPER

4 tbsp coconut oil
2 dried red chilies
1/2 tsp asafoetida or crushed fennel seeds
1 1/2 tsp black mustard seeds
2-3 sprigs of curry leaves

FOR THE KORMA

1/2 cup tomato puree
1 tsp ground turmeric
1 tbsp ground coriander
1/4 cup dried cranberries (page 205)
1 medium onion, chopped
1/2 cup thickly sliced carrots
1/2 cup chopped zucchini or eggplant
1 cup roughly chopped bell pepper
1/2 cup green beans, cut in 1-inch pieces
1 cup sliced mushrooms
1 cup diced celeriac
1/2 cup cauliflower, cut in small florets
4 oz halloumi or paneer, cubed, browned
1/4 cup powdered sweetener
1 tsp salt

Our first foray into Indian cooking was a simple yet tasty butter chicken, paired with a veggie curry, or Nine Gem Korma, so named for the nine elements (fruits, nuts, and vegetables) in the dish. Its traditional spices—as well as the vegetables used—vary from region to region and from household to household. Every family (and restaurant) has its own secret recipe.

Tempering or *tadka*, as it is known in Hindi, is the act of heating and blooming spices in hot oil to enhance the flavours. The tempered spices can be added to the curry at the beginning or the end but adding them at the end intensifies the flavours. We suggest pouring the temper on the curry tableside.

Use celeriac instead of potato, dried cranberries instead of raisins, and almonds instead of higher-carb cashews.

To prepare the spice blend
Toast the spices to intensify the flavour. Place all the ingredients in a large dry sauté pan and cook on a low heat until fragrant. Transfer to a blender and blend to a fine powder. Set aside.

To prepare the curry paste
Place the garlic, ginger, and green chilies in a food processor and pulse to a paste. Add water if the paste is too thick to puree. Set aside.

To prepare the temper
Heat the oil in a large sauté pan on a medium heat. Choose a deep pan if possible, as the seeds will pop and sizzle. Add 1/4 teaspoon asafoetida and 1 teaspoon black mustard seeds. When the mustard seeds start to pop, add 2 to 3 sprigs of curry leaves and cook until fragrant. (Remove from the heat if doing this step at the end.)

To assemble
Place the oil and onion in a large sauté pan and cook until the onion is soft and almost translucent, about 5 minutes. Add the chili paste, tomato, turmeric, and coriander, as well as 1 to 2 tablespoons spice blend, and cook until the oil separates. Add the vegetables and toss to ensure that all are coated, then cook until fragrant, about 2 to 3 minutes. Add the sweetener and salt and adjust the seasoning. Add 2 1/2 cups water and simmer until the vegetables are cooked through and the liquid has reduced to a thick gravy, about 20 minutes.

Whole Roasted Cauliflower

1 whole head cauliflower, outer stems and leaves removed
1/4 cup olive oil
1 tbsp red wine vinegar or white balsamic vinegar
1 tsp smoked paprika
1 tsp salt
1 tsp garlic powder
1 tsp Korean chili flakes
1 tsp ground cumin
1/2 tsp dried parsley
1/2 tsp dried thyme
1/2 tsp pepper

This dish is so simple that you're just not gonna believe it!

Start the cooking process in the microwave so that the cauliflower is cooked through in time for the outside to be crisped up.

1. Preheat the oven to 400°F and line a baking sheet with parchment paper.
2. Microwave the cauliflower on high for 8 to 10 minutes or until tender, then place the whole cauliflower on the prepared baking sheet.
3. Combine all the other seasoning ingredients in a small mixing bowl.
4. Rub the seasoning on the cauliflower and roast for 30 minutes or until the outside is slightly crispy and a dark golden brown.

Fish Entrées

Born down by the Water...

Blackened Salmon
Cod in Tarragon Butter
Crispy Caesar Salmon
Fish Stick Tacos
Lemon and Dill Baked Cod
Piccata Style Trout with Capers
Salmon en Papillote
Soused Shrimp
Turmeric-Crusted Cod with Tomato Jam

We grew up next to the water. We were taught at a very young age to be wary of the ever-moving majestic blue beast that is the Atlantic Ocean. As beautiful and bountiful as she is, that vast body of water is to be respected: what was calm and serene one minute could be bitter and life-threatening the next.

I think the proximity (of the sea) and abundance of seafood meant we didn't eat it often in our household and the thought of ordering fish in a fancy restaurant was preposterous. Why would I order that when I could make that myself at home? I suppose it all comes back to the theory that what we want most are those things that we cannot have. In other words, there wasn't a lot of seafood in my earlier days.

Local food sustainability and accessibility are topics that were not on our radars back then but today they are top of mind. I've learned to expand my horizons and also look closer to home for sustenance. Food ingredients closer to home and closer to the earth and ocean are my choice these days.

Blackened Salmon

4 6-oz salmon fillet portions

FOR THE DRY MIX
1 tbsp paprika
1 tsp brown sweetener
1 tsp salt
1 tsp onion powder
1 tsp garlic powder
1/2 tsp pepper
1/2 tsp dried thyme
1/2 tsp cayenne (optional)

TO FINISH
2 tbsp butter
2 tbsp fresh dill
1 tsp fresh lemon thyme

This recipe was born on the grill on a warm and sultry night in our backyard in Topsail.

Summers are all about outdoor living, getting out there and soaking up every single moment of sunshine and warmer weather while we can. On this night, we mixed up spices by the light of the moon and threw the coated salmon (and the sides) on the blacktop grill and then ate it under the summer sky.

Blackened Salmon is not burned; it gets its colour from the cooked spice mix, particularly the paprika. The oils help to caramelize the spices, giving the outside its deep coppery, almost black hue, while the inside of the salmon stays moist and is perfectly cooked.

1. Whisk all the dry mix ingredients together in a small bowl. Set aside.
2. Pat the salmon dry with a paper towel. Sprinkle half of the dry mix on the salmon.
3. Heat the oil in a large cast-iron sauté pan on a medium-high heat. Lay the salmon pieces in the hot pan, coated side down. Place them away from you so any splattered oil is deflected away. Sear the salmon without moving it for about 3 minutes, or until the flesh is cooked about one-third of the way up the pieces.
4. While the salmon is cooking, sprinkle the other half of the dry mix on it. Flip the salmon and reduce the heat to medium low. Cook, without moving the salmon, until both sides are blackened and its internal temperature is 125°F.

NOTE: Do not let the temperature of the salmon reach more than 130°F while it is in the pan. It will continue to cook after it is removed from the pan. If it is left in the pan too long, it will dry out and be overcooked.

FISH ENTRÉES | 133

Cod in Tarragon Butter

FOR THE TARRAGON BUTTER
2 tbsp butter, at room temperature
2 tsp dried tarragon
1 tsp garlic powder

FOR THE FISH
1 tbsp oil
2 6-oz cod fillets
1 tsp salt
1/2 tsp pepper
1/2 cup cherry tomatoes, halved

Growing up on the east coast meant I didn't encounter a wide range of spices: salt, pepper, and onion and garlic powders were as exotic as things got.

My palate and pantry matured as was I exposed to the world and its vast cultures—but it wasn't until we visited France that I fell in love with tarragon, which was the flavour profile for a fish course. I loved it.

1. Use a spatula or spoon to combine all the tarragon butter ingredients, and set aside.
2. Season the cod evenly with the salt and pepper. Heat a sauté pan on a medium heat. Coat the pan with the oil. Place the cod fillets seasoned side down and cook for 3 minutes.
3. Add the tarragon butter to the pan and allow it to melt. Gently flip the cod and add the tomatoes. Cook 3 to 4 minutes longer (or until the cod begins to flake easily) while spooning the tarragon butter over it.
4. Transfer the cod to a plate and return the pan with the tomatoes to the heat and cook until the tomatoes have softened outside and released most of their juices, about 2 minutes.
5. Spoon the tomato and herbed butter on the cod.

FISH ENTRÉES | 135

Crispy Caesar Salmon

FOR THE CAESAR DRESSING

1 cup oil, try 1/2 cup light tasting olive oil and 1/2 cup avocado oil
4 oz grated Parmesan cheese, plus more for garnish
1 tbsp white balsamic vinegar
1 tbsp lemon juice
1 tbsp yellow mustard
5-8 cloves garlic, grated
1 tsp fish sauce
1 tsp salt
1 tsp pepper
1 large egg
1 tbsp nutritional yeast
1 tsp dried parsley

FOR THE SALMON

1 cup crushed pork rinds or almond flour
4 oz grated Parmesan cheese
1 tsp dried parsley
1/2 tsp dried thyme or tarragon
1/2 tsp Korean chili flakes
1/2 tsp pepper
4 6-8 oz salmon pieces
1/4 cup Caesar dressing (recipe above)

Learning to batch-cook and using the take-out-of-the-freezer or refrigerator option is a game changer for many families. Increasing the yield by doubling or tripling a recipe will save time down the road. This recipe fits the bill. Our (often leftover) homemade Caesar dressing is the perfect flavour enhancer for the salmon.

To prepare the Caesar dressing

Put all the ingredients except the egg, yeast, and parsley in a tall narrow jar or the vessel of an immersion blender and blend to fully incorporate. Add the egg, nutritional yeast, and parsley and allow the egg to sink to the bottom, then place the immersion blender on the bottom, and blend. As the dressing thickens at the bottom, slowly move the blender up through the mixture. Blend up and down until all the oil has been incorporated into the dressing.

To assemble

1. Preheat the oven to 350°F.
2. Combine the dry ingredients and then the cheese in a small mixing bowl. Mix well and set aside.
3. Dry the salmon pieces and place them in a greased 13- by 9-inch baking dish. Use the back of a spoon or a rubber spatula to spread the Caesar dressing on the salmon. Sprinkle the dry mixture on the salmon, pressing gently into the dressing.
4. Bake uncovered for 20 minutes or until the salmon flakes easily with a fork.
5. Broil for the last few minutes for a crispier crust. Watch carefully to ensure that it does not burn.

NOTE: Try this on chicken. Increase the cooking time until the chicken reaches an internal temperature of 165°F.

Fish Stick Tacos
➤ **EXTRA: SOFT TORTILLA WRAPS**

1 lb cod, sea bass, halibut, or any white fish
1 large egg, whisked
1/2 cup water

FOR THE DREDGE

1 cup crushed pork rinds or almond flour
6 oz grated Parmesan cheese
1/2 tsp garlic powder
1/2 tsp paprika
1/2 tsp dried thyme
1/2 tsp dried tarragon
1/2 tsp salt
1/4 tsp pepper

FOR THE HARD TORTILLA SHELLS

1 cup almond flour
4 tbsp psyllium husk
1 tbsp egg white powder
1 tbsp coconut flour
1 tsp xanthan gum
1/2 tsp salt
1 tbsp oil
1 tbsp apple cider or white vinegar
1 large egg
1 tbsp whipping cream

FOR THE SLAW

1 cup finely shredded red cabbage
1/4 cup shredded carrot
1/2 cup chopped fresh parsley, basil, or cilantro
1/2 cup chopped fresh tarragon, or 1 tsp dried tarragon
1/4 cup thinly sliced onion

Fish sticks always make me smile; they remind me of my son. He hated fish when he was little. He loved chicken nuggets though, which worked to my benefit as a mom trying to nourish her finicky kid. Presto, chango ... fish sticks became "special" chicken nuggets. Special because he never realized it was fish sticks cut into pieces. He gobbled them up as quickly as he could, licking his fingers every single time.

Now that he's older he thinks he doesn't like fish again, but I'm willing to bet that in a blind taste test he would still love Mom's special chicken nuggets especially when they're all wrapped up in taco goodness.

Try these fish sticks by themselves, as simple fish tacos with Mayonnaise (page 272) or fully dressed with the slaw and salsa as described here.

To prepare the fish sticks
1. Preheat the oven to 375°F and line a baking sheet with parchment paper.
2. Cut the fish in strips and remove any bones. Pat dry with a paper towel and set aside.
3. Whisk the eggs and water in a medium flat-bottomed bowl. In a shallow dish, combine the pork rinds, cheese, and spices.
4. Use a fork and spoon to dip each piece of fish into the egg mixture, then press into the dredge. Ensure that both sides are coated. Gently shake off any excess and lay the coated fish on the prepared baking sheet in a single layer. Drizzle with the oil and bake for 15 to 20 minutes, depending on the thickness of the fish. While the fish sticks are baking, prepare the tortillas and slaw.

To prepare the hard tortilla shells
1. Whisk the dry ingredients together and set aside. Whisk the egg in a medium bowl.
2. Add the dry mixture to the eggs and then add all remaining ingredients, adding the water in increments to achieve the desired consistency: a looser batter will make a thin wrap; thicker batter will result in a slightly thicker wrap. Whisk to incorporate or use a blender to ensure a lump-free batter.
3. Pour the batter onto a 9-inch silicone mat or a flat dinner plate, and microwave for 90 seconds or until most of the tortilla is dry.
4. Run a spatula around the edge of the wrap to carefully lift it from the silicone mat. Using a cutting board as a base, and your hand on one side and a large spatula or knife on the other, form the tortilla shell and hold for about 30 seconds until the shell cools and hardens.

FOR THE SLAW DRESSING

1/4 cup oil

2 tbsp sour cream

2 tbsp lime juice or apple cider vinegar

1 tbsp mayonnaise (page 272)

1 tbsp Dijon mustard

1 tbsp chili garlic sauce

1 tbsp powdered sweetener

2 cloves garlic minced, or 1 tsp garlic powder

1 tsp paprika

1 tsp salt

1/2 tsp pepper

1/2 tsp ground cumin

1/4 tsp ground coriander

FOR THE SALSA (OPTIONAL)

2 tomatoes, diced

2 spring onions, sliced

1 jalapeño pepper, diced (optional)

1/2 small garlic clove, minced

1/4 cup roughly chopped fresh parsley or cilantro

2 tbsp lime juice

2 tbsp olive oil

pinch of ground cumin

TO GARNISH

avocado slices

chopped fresh cilantro, tarragon, or parsley

feta cheese

lime wedges

sliced olives

guacamole

To prepare the slaw and dressing

Place all the dressing ingredients in a Mason jar and shake to mix. Place all the slaw ingredients in a medium glass bowl and toss. Set both aside until you are ready to eat.

To prepare the salsa

Mix all the ingredients in a medium glass bowl and toss to evenly coat.

To assemble

1. Place all the slaw ingredients in a medium bowl and add the dressing. Toss to evenly coat.
2. Place a spoonful of slaw in the bottom of a tortilla shell, then add the fish sticks and salsa, if using. Add garnishes as desired.

NOTE: To fry the fish sticks, place about 3 tablespoons oil in a deep sauté pan. Fry in small batches until golden brown. Never leave the oil unattended.

▶ SOFT TORTILLA WRAPS

1 tsp coconut flour

2 tbsp coconut flour

1 tbsp psyllium husk

2 tbsp egg white powder

1/4 tsp salt

2 large eggs, at room temperature

2 tbsp whipping cream

1 tsp-1 tbsp water

Follow the cooking instructions for the hard shell tortillas and, instead of forming them, lay them flat on a cooling rack to dry.

Lemon and Dill Baked Cod

1 medium onion, partially cooked, sliced
4 8-oz pieces skinless cod fillets
1 tsp salt
1/2 tsp pepper
1/2 tsp garlic powder
1 lemon, sliced

FOR THE LEMON BUTTER MIX

1 tbsp chopped fresh dill,
    or 1 tsp dried dill
3 tbsp vegetable or fish broth
1/4 cup butter, melted
3 cloves garlic, minced and mashed
zest of 1 lemon
1 tbsp lemon juice

8-10 cherry tomatoes, for garnish

This simple baked cod dish is delicately flavoured with dill and lemon. Bake as individual servings or line a pan with these ingredients and bake as a family-style casserole.

Try it with the optional batter—but first try without to enjoy the simplicity of the fish and lemon.

1. Microwave the onion slices and 2 tablespoons water until translucent and starting to soften.
2. Preheat the oven to 375°F.
3. Pat the cod dry with a paper towel and set aside.
4. Mix the lemon butter ingredients together and set aside.
5. Place the onion in an oven-safe casserole dish and layer the lemon on the onion so that each piece of cod is in contact with at least one piece of lemon. Place the cod on the onion and lemon. Season with the salt, pepper, and garlic powder.
6. Pour the lemon butter on the cod and place the tomatoes around the edges of the cod.
7. Bake for 15 to 20 minutes. Do not overcook or the cod will dry out. Remove from the oven and plate, spooning pan juices on the finished dish.

NOTE: Zest 1 lemon and place the zestless lemon under the cod.

✔ **TIP**

Try this cod lightly coated with 1/2 cup almond flour, 1 teaspoon paprika, 1 teaspoon garlic powder, 1 teaspoon salt, and 1/2 teaspoon pepper. Use an egg wash to help the coating stick.

FISH ENTRÉES | 143

Piccata Style Trout WITH CAPERS

2 tbsp oil
3 6-oz thin, boneless trout fillets
1 tsp salt
1 tsp garlic powder
1/2 tsp pepper
2 tbsp butter
2 tbsp capers
2 tbsp dry white wine
1 tbsp lemon juice

fresh parsley, to garnish

It's August and we're in terrific company. After participating in a foodie event surrounded by several chefs from across Canada, we're enjoying each other's company, a fire, and a libation.

One of our colleagues returned from the nearby river with his prize of freshly caught trout and things really started to get interesting.

The fireside show was mesmerizing. Watching the metallic glow as chef spooned the pan juices over the fish in the cast-iron pan while bathed in firelight was a thing of beauty.

And the trout was the best I've ever tasted. It was devoured with gusto. I hope you and your family enjoy my version of this epic meal just as much as we did.

1. Place the oil in a large sauté pan on a medium-high heat.
2. Season both sides of the trout with the salt, garlic powder, and pepper. When the oil is hot, add the trout skin side down. Add the butter, capers, and white wine and use a tablespoon to carefully spoon the pan juices on the trout.
3. Cook until the skin turns golden brown, then flip the trout. Leave the trout flesh side down for about 20 to 30 seconds, then flip it back to skin side down. Remove the pan from the heat, add the lemon juice, and spoon the pan juices on the trout one last time.
4. Transfer to a plate.

NOTE: Whisk 1/4 cup dry white wine into the pan juices to create a pan sauce. Try this recipe with any fish or meat but vary the cooking time appropriately. Finish any meatier cuts in the oven.

Did you know?
The Italian word *piccata* means larded, but traced further into culinary history it seems to be a translation of the French word *pique*, meaning sharp or piquant. It refers to delicate slices of meat or fish sautéed in a buttery pan with lemon juice, white wine, and capers.

FISH ENTRÉES | 145

Salmon en Papillote

fennel stalks and fronds, chopped about 1/4-1/2 inch thick
1/2 medium onion, sliced
1/8 cup water
2 deboned salmon pieces, seasoned with 1 tsp salt and 1/2 tsp pepper
2 tomatoes, roughly chopped
1/4 cup lemon juice
4 tbsp olive oil

extra fennel fronds, for garnish

Baking in parchment paper is one of the most forgiving ways to prepare fish—but also the most unnerving. Because the juices and spices are sealed inside with the fish, it will be juicy, tender, and tasty. The trick is getting the meal cooked to perfection and knowing when the fish is done but not overdone.

Precook any other add-ins before adding them to the papillote as the fish is delicate and cooks quickly; it will overcook if left long enough for the onion or other vegetables to cook. Serve these to guests in individual parchment packets.

The recipe is written for two single packets, but the yield can be increased by doubling or tripling the recipe to match the number of dinner guests.

1. Preheat the oven to 350°F.
2. Place the fennel stalks, onion, and water in a microwave-safe bowl and cook on high for about 2 minutes to soften and partially cook both. When the vegetables start to turn translucent and soften, remove them from the microwave and set aside to cool.
3. Tear off two 20-inch-long sheets of parchment paper and fold each in half. Place the open parchment pieces on a baking sheet.
4. Working on one side of the parchment paper toward the centre fold, layer the fennel fronds to create a bed for the salmon on each sheet. Place the cooled fennel stalks and onion and the tomato pieces on the greens. This bed of aromatics infuses directly into the salmon. When the vegetables have been arranged, place the salmon on the aromatics. Drizzle with the lemon juice and olive oil and sprinkle with the remaining fennel fronds.
5. Seal the parchment pieces by folding the parchment in half again and crimping the edge until the packets are completely sealed. Transfer the baking sheet to the oven. Bake until the parchment puffs and the liquid inside the packet bubbles, about 25 to 30 minutes.
6. Let the packets rest 5 minutes before opening them.

NOTE: Look for already-sealed parchment bags. Add the ingredients and fold to close. Partially cook the fennel stalks and onion in advance.

Be mindful
Make sure to tell your guests to be careful of escaping steam when they open their packets!

Soused Shrimp

❖ **VARIATION: CURRY SHRIMP**

2 tsp oil
1 tsp fish sauce
6 garlic cloves, minced
1 tsp Korean chili flakes
1 tsp salt
1 tsp sweetener
1/2 tsp pepper
1/2 cup white wine
1/4 cup fish broth
juice from 1 lemon
1 lb large or jumbo shrimp, peeled and deveined
2 tsp butter

fresh parsley, for garnish (optional)

This recipe focuses on getting the sauce up and running before adding the shrimp. Shrimp needs only a quick flash in the pan or it becomes rubbery.

Allow plenty of time to cook the wine off, season to perfection, tweaking and adding/subtracting seasoning to suit your own palate, and only then give the shrimp their time in the soused sauce.

This buttery garlic shrimp will be ready in under 20 minutes. Perfect for unexpected guests!

1. Heat the olive oil in a skillet on a medium heat. Add all the ingredients except the butter, shrimp, and parsley. Bring to a boil, then reduce the heat to medium and cook for another 2 to 3 minutes. Reduce the heat to low and check the seasoning. When the desired flavour and consistency of the sauce have been reached, add the shrimp, and cook, stirring for 2 to 3 minutes until opaque. Do not overcook the shrimp. Remove it to a side plate.
2. Whisk the butter into the pan juices and increase to a medium-high heat to reduce and finish the sauce.
3. Pour the finished sauce over the shrimp and garnish with the parsley.

NOTE: The shrimp will continue to cook on the plate and in the hot broth. It is best to err on the side of slightly undercooked rather than overcooked. Chicken or vegetable broth may be substituted for the fish broth.

❖ **VARIATION: CURRY SHRIMP**

Substitute an equal amount of canned tomatoes for the wine and broth for the coconut milk. Add 1 teaspoon curry powder, 1/2 teaspoon garam masala, 1/2 teaspoon ground ginger, and 1/4 teaspoon ground coriander. Continue with the instructions above.

Turmeric-Crusted Cod WITH TOMATO JAM

1 lb cod or other white fish (sea bass or halibut)
1 tsp salt
1/2 tsp pepper

FOR THE TURMERIC PASTE
2 oz grated Parmesan cheese
3 tbsp oil
2 tbsp turmeric
1 tbsp coconut sauce
1 tbsp grated fresh ginger, or 1 tsp ground ginger
1 tsp dried parsley
1 tsp dried dill
1/2 tsp salt
1/2 tsp pepper
1/4 tsp ground coriander
3 cloves garlic, crushed into a paste (use a mortar and pestle)

FOR THE TOMATO JAM
1 tbsp oil
6 oz cherry tomatoes
1/2 tsp Korean chili flakes or alternate heat
1 clove garlic, minced and mashed
1 tsp roughly chopped fresh cilantro or parsley

The whole world seems to have caught on to the medicinal healing powers of turmeric. Turmeric is a well-known powerful anti-inflammatory and an antioxidant that may even help ward off cancer. Turmeric pills, powders, and pastes have been created to help get turmeric into your body.

Our view is to always eat nutrients in the purest form. In this case, however, more is involved than just adding it to food. Curcumin, the active ingredient that provides the health boost in turmeric, is not bioavailable, that is, our body has difficulty absorbing it. Pepper makes it easier for curcumin to pass through the intestinal wall into the bodies.

1. Line a baking sheet with parchment paper and preheat the oven to 375°F.
2. Season the cod with the salt, pepper, and lime juice and place it on the prepared baking sheet. Set aside.
3. Combine the turmeric paste ingredients in a medium glass bowl and mix well. Use a spatula to spread it on the cod. Bake for 20 to 25 minutes or until it is opaque and flakes easily. Remove from the pan and set aside to rest. Baking time depends on the thickness of the cod.
4. While the cod is resting, make the tomato jam: Heat the oil in a small saucepan on a medium heat. Add the tomatoes and spices and sauté until the tomatoes are soft. Spoon a dollop of the finished jam on the baked cod tableside.

Meat Entrées

My Heart Craves Protein...

Braised Beef Ribs and Daikon
Cheesy Beef Bake / Taco Pie
Chicken à la King
Chicken Lombardy
Creamy Carbonara Primavera with Bacon
Egg Roll in a Bowl
Grilled Spatchcock Chicken with Maple Garlic and Cinco de Mayo BBQ Sauces
Honey-ish Balsamic Pork Chops
Lemon Chicken
Masala-Spiced Pork Chops
Mongolian Beef
OMJ Half-Baked Chicken
Pork Chops with Mushroom Ragout
Pork Chops with Irish Whiskey Sauce
Red Pepper Meatloaf
Roasted-Garlic-and-Parm-Crusted Pork
Seared Duck Breast with Cherry Gastrique
Shepherd's Pie
Slow-Roasted Maple Pork Loin with Sun-Dried Tomatoes and Mushrooms
Stuffed Polpette al Sugo—Meatballs in Red Sauce

It is important to ensure that you are getting lots of clean protein—not shakes and protein bars, but protein found in real food such as fish and meat. The closer you can get to farm fresh, food with no additives, the better it is for your body. Quality in food matters, especially with protein.

Our bodies get essential amino and fatty acids from protein. Without sufficient protein intake, your body will consume its own: your muscles. This is an especially serious concern when you consider that the heart is a muscle.

Protein is the most necessary macronutrient for human life; amino acids assist in nearly every bodily process, including building and repairing our bodies.

The protein leverage hypothesis suggests that you will keep craving foods until the protein requirements are met, even if sufficient calories have been consumed for the day. This is why it is easy to overeat high-carb foods and almost impossible to overeat chicken or beef. Your body will tell you that it has had enough ... if you're listening. When you consume enough high-quality protein, you feel full and satisfied, making it less likely to overeat and snack between meals.

Give your heart what it desires. Protect your muscles and especially your heart. Eat lots of protein with these satisfying recipes.

Braised Beef Ribs and Daikon

6-8 mushrooms
2 tbsp oil, and more as needed
2 lb short beef ribs, cut in sections between the bones
2 tsp chili garlic sauce
2-inch piece of ginger, cut in thick matchsticks
8 cloves garlic, smashed
1 tbsp brown sweetener
1 tbsp powdered sweetener
2 carrots, sliced diagonally
2 cups broth
3 cups water
1/2 cup coconut sauce
1/4 cup apple cider vinegar
1 cup red wine
2 tsp Ceylon cinnamon
1/2 tsp ground cardamom
1/4 tsp nutmeg
1 tsp fennel seeds, crushed
2 daikon, cut in 1-1 1/2-inch-thick rounds
8 spring onions, cut in 2-inch lengths, white sections only (reserve greens for garnish)
3-4 sprigs of fresh thyme
drizzle of cold-pressed sesame oil

I have a confession. I have a little fascination with fondant potatoes. There's something about those (in our world) faux-tatoes that are perfectly cooked, soft on the inside yet crispy and crunchy on the outside.

I've often thought about trying to recreate the fondant concept with celeriac, but the thought of cutting perfect rings with cutters and discarding the rest of the perfectly good veg doesn't jive with me.

But why not try small daikon radish? They're already round and will take on any flavour.

We pull the daikon into service here as faux-tato. If you cook these vegetables in a red wine sauce long enough, they take on the hue of the sauce. You can also remove the daikon pieces from the pot and fry them until they are crispy and crunchy to add to the texture.

1. Heat a wide-based sauté pan or Dutch oven on a high heat. When the pan is hot, add the oil, then add the beef ribs and cook until they are browned on all sides and caramelized. Work in small batches and do not crowd the pan. If the ribs are resistant to being moved in the pan, they are not cooked yet. Cook for a while longer and when they are properly seared, they will easily release from the pan.
2. Transfer the ribs to a bowl when the first batch is done and continue with any remaining ribs.
3. When the ribs are cooked and set aside, deglaze the pan by adding the broth, wine, vinegar, water, cinnamon, nutmeg, and cardamom and bring it to a boil. Cook for about 15 to 20 minutes until the sauce has slightly reduced. Turn off the heat and cool slightly.
4. Preheat the oven to 400°F.
5. Return the beef to the pan and add the chili garlic sauce. Cook for 1 minute, while stirring to coat each rib piece in the sauce. Add the ginger, garlic, and carrot, and top up with water until the ribs are almost totally covered in the liquid. Tuck the fresh herb pieces around the ribs. If using dried herbs, sprinkle them on the ribs. Cover and place the pan in the hot oven and immediately reduce the temperature to 275°F.
6. While the ribs are cooking, place the daikon in a hot sauté pan and sear for a few minutes. This step is optional but it adds flavour and colour to the vegetables. After the ribs have cooked for 1 hour, place the daikon around the ribs. Cook the ribs for another 2 hours or until the beef is soft and tender and the daikon is fork-tender. Remove the ribs from the pan to a bowl. Drizzle sesame oil on the ribs.
7. Garnish with the green onion tops.

NOTE: Olive oil can be used instead of cold-pressed sesame oil. Cool any extra broth and freeze it in small portioned, flat-frozen freezer bags for future use. This broth that can be used in any recipe. A portion of this broth can be reduced to provide a sauce for the ribs.

MEAT ENTRÉES | 155

Cheesy Beef Bake / Taco Pie

FOR THE BASE

6 slices bacon, cut in 1-inch squares
1 lb ground beef
1 medium onion, diced
4 cloves garlic, minced
1 cup chopped spinach
1/2 cup diced bell pepper
4-6 mushrooms, diced
2 tbsp coconut sauce
1 tsp fish sauce
1 tsp dried thyme
1 tsp ground cumin
1 tsp ground coriander
1 tsp chili powder
1 tsp salt
1/2 tsp pepper

FOR THE SAUCE

1/4 cup whipping cream or sour cream
3 large eggs
6 oz grated cheddar cheese
2 tsp Korean chili flakes or paprika
1 tsp dried parsley
1 tsp garlic powder

The traditional version of this recipe is usually found with layers of corn chips or flour wraps. These fillers and carbs do not add flavour, but instead add bulk to our waists!

This taco pie is delicious on its own, but try it dressed as a taco. Add shredded lettuce, chopped tomatoes, guacamole, salsa, and/or sour cream in a garnish-your-own main meal event.

1. Place the bacon, beef, and onion in a large sauté pan on a medium heat and cook until the beef has browned. Add the remaining ingredients and stir. Transfer the beef mixture to a baking or casserole dish.
2. Preheat the oven to 350°F.
3. Mix the sauce ingredients together in a medium mixing bowl and then stir into the beef mixture. Bake for 30 to 40 minutes.
4. Allow this dish to cool before serving, as the cheese will be molten hot.

NOTE: Add 4 tablespoons Cancun spice mix (page 166) instead of the spices in the base, then top with sour cream, lime juice, shredded lettuce, chopped tomatoes, guacamole, and salsa as desired.

MEAT ENTRÉES | 157

Chicken à la King

- 3 tbsp butter
- 1 medium onion, diced
- 1/2 cup diced red bell pepper
- 3 cloves garlic, minced
- 1/2 cup diced green beans, cut in 1-inch pieces
- 4 oz mushrooms, sliced
- 1/4 cup apple cider vinegar
- 2 cups chicken broth
- 4 cups cubed, cooked chicken
- 1 tsp salt
- 3/4 tsp pepper
- 1 1/2 tsp paprika
- 1/4 tsp nutmeg
- 1 tsp mustard powder
- 1 tsp dried tarragon
- 1/2 cup whipping cream
- 2 oz cream cheese
- 2 large egg yolks
- 1/4–1/2 tsp xanthan gum
- 1 package shirataki or konjac noodles (optional)

This recipe works well as a simple baked noodle casserole dish or a crust-covered pie. As with any recipe that includes carb replacements, always remember that these items add up fast. Remove the noodles and eat the delicious chicken stew as it is, to your heart's content. If using noodles or pastry, portions should be limited—try serving a brightly garnished green salad with a small serving of Chicken à la King on the side, to keep the carb count down.

1. Place the butter in a large oven-safe sauté pan on a medium-high heat. Add the onion and cook for about 3 minutes, or until it starts to turn translucent. Add the pepper and mushrooms, and cook for 2 more minutes. Add the green beans and garlic. Let the vegetables cook until they are almost soft, about 3 to 5 minutes, depending on their size. Add the vinegar to deglaze the pan. Use a wooden spoon to get all the browned bits off the bottom of the pan. Add the broth, cooked chicken, and spices, and stir to incorporate. Remove from the heat and set aside.
2. Meanwhile, heat the cream and cream cheese in a medium saucepan.
3. Place the eggs in a medium mixing bowl and whisk.
4. Remove the cream from the heat. Using a 1-cup measure, remove a portion of the hot cream. Working very slowly, drizzle the cup of hot cream into the eggs while whisking. If this is drizzled too quickly, the warm cream will cook the eggs. Whisk the egg/cream mixture back into the saucepan of hot cream. Whisk in the xanthan gum. The sauce will thicken as it cools. More xanthan gum can be added before plating if the thickness needs to be adjusted.
5. Transfer the cream mixture to the pan with the vegetables and noodles and stir. Place the filled pan in a preheated 375°F oven and bake for 15 to 20 minutes. Remove from the oven and let cool.

NOTE: Sprinkle 1/2 teaspoon chopped fresh parsley and a pinch of Korean chili flakes on the top to add extra colour to the plate. Batch-cook the chicken on the grill or a baking sheet in the oven. With a thin coating of oil, salt, and pepper, they are ready to transform into any weeknight meal. Noodles can be replaced with a thin crust over the chicken and vegetable mixture. Try the pie crust (page 56) and cut discs with a glass or cut basic strips about 1 by 3 inches. Bake and then stand them on the edge of a serving plate as a garnish.

Chicken Lombardy

❖ **VARIATION: MARSALA CREAM CHICKEN**

FOR THE DREDGE
1/2 cup almond flour
1/4 cup coconut flour
1 tsp salt
1 tsp garlic powder
1/2 tsp pepper

FOR THE EGG WASH
1 large egg
1/4 cup water

FOR THE CHICKEN
3 boneless, skinless chicken breasts, sliced lengthwise, seasoned with salt and pepper
1/3 cup butter

FOR THE SAUCE
2 tbsp oil
4 oz mushrooms, thickly sliced
1 tbsp butter
3/4 cup dry red wine
1/2 cup chicken stock
1/2 tsp salt
1/4 tsp pepper

TO GARNISH/FINISH
4 oz grated mozzarella cheese
4 oz grated Parmesan cheese
2 green onions, sliced

In this decadent dish, chicken breasts have been drenched in masala or dry red wine. Chicken Lombardy, Chicken Marsala, or Drunken Chicken are all similar and delicious. This is our nod to the French classic of coq au vin.

This chicken can be done without the dredge for a quicker and easier option but try it as intended at least once.

Allow time for the wine to cook off; for an alcohol-free version, use broth and vinegar instead of the wine.

To prepare the dredged chicken
1. Mix the flours, salt, garlic, and pepper.
2. Whisk together the egg and water for the egg wash.
3. Use a fork to dip the chicken into the egg wash and then into the dredge. Press the chicken into the dry mix with a spoon and gently shake to remove any excess coating. Set aside and continue coating any remaining pieces.
4. Preheat the oven to 450°F. Grease a casserole dish or Dutch oven large enough to hold all the chicken pieces with ample room.
5. Heat the oil in a large sauté pan on a medium-high heat. Add the mushrooms and cook, stirring frequently, until they begin to brown; remove and set aside. Add the butter to the pan. When the butter has melted, and working in batches, brown the chicken on both sides. Remove from the heat and place the chicken breasts in the prepared dish. Set aside.
6. Reserve the drippings for the Lombardy sauce.

To prepare the sauce
Whisk all the sauce ingredients in the same pan. Bring to a boil, reduce the heat, and simmer uncovered for 10 minutes. Set aside.

To assemble
1. Sprinkle the mushrooms evenly on the chicken. Pour the sauce on the chicken. Mix the cheeses and sprinkle directly on the chicken pieces.
2. Cover and bake for 20 to 25 minutes, until the cheese has melted and the chicken has reached an internal temperature of 165°F. Remove from the oven and sprinkle the green onion on the top.

NOTE: Wine can be substituted for 1/2 cup broth/water and 1/4 cup vinegar. If white wine is used instead of red, the colour of the sauce is less intense.

❖ **VARIATION: MARSALA CREAM CHICKEN**
Substitute the broth with 1/2 cup whipping cream. Whisk in 1 tablespoon Dijon mustard; 1 medium onion, sliced; 2 garlic cloves, diced; and 3 sprigs of fresh thyme, and continue according to the instructions above.

Creamy Carbonara Primavera WITH BACON

1 tsp olive oil or butter
6 slices thick-cut bacon, or 1/2 lb pancetta, cut in 1/2-inch strips
1 medium onion, roughly chopped
4-6 mushrooms, thickly sliced
1 cup chopped greens such as spinach or romaine lettuce
2 garlic cloves, minced
1/2 bell pepper, cut in 1-inch squares
2 large eggs
6 oz grated Parmesan or pecorino cheese
1 package shirataki or konjac pasta, or spiralized vegetable noodles
1/2 tsp salt
1/4 tsp pepper
1 tsp dried parsley
1/4-1/2 cup broth, if needed

I wouldn't have eaten this dish in my younger years. Raw egg as a sauce? Sure, that can't be fit to eat!

But when you know that the secret to carbonara is the tempered eggs, it's not so scary. Tempered eggs have long been part of east coast cooking—nans or moms making an old-fashioned custard or pudding would have tempered their eggs to get the results they needed. You have to temper eggs really slowly. This is where intuitive cooking comes in; you have to react to what you see in front of you. Drizzle and whisk. Drizzle and whisk. It's a dance between too fast and too slow.

While you're tempering the eggs, we recommend not only turning off the heat under the pot but taking the pot off the element altogether. Be ever so patient and know that you are creating a masterpiece your entire family will love.

1. Place the oil in a large sauté pan on a medium-high heat. Add the bacon and onion and cook until the onion is translucent and the bacon is cooked through. Add the garlic and cook 1 minute, then add the peppers.
2. While the peppers are cooking, combine the eggs and half of the cheese in a small bowl.
3. Add the mushrooms to the pan and cook until they start to brown on the edges. Add the greens and cook until wilted. Add the noodles, season with salt and pepper, and stir to incorporate.
4. Remove the pan from the heat and allow to cool slightly. Slowly drizzle and stir the egg/cheese mixture into the pan. The secret is to allow the pasta to cool enough so that it will not curdle the eggs but hot enough to help the eggs come together to make a creamy carbonara sauce. Toss to combine. Add the second half of the cheese and sprinkle with the parsley to finish.
5. If the noodles have cooled too much while mixing, turn the pan on low for 1 minute, being careful not to break the sauce.

NOTE: Remove the hot pan from the heat when tempering. Broth may be added at the end to stretch the sauce. If the sauce breaks, this dish will still taste good.

Egg Roll in a Bowl
❖ **WITH VARIATIONS**

2 tbsp oil
1 medium onion, diced
1 lb ground beef, chicken,
  or pork (or 2/3 beef and 1/3 pork)
1 tsp salt, or to taste
1 tsp dried parsley
1/2 tsp dried thyme
1/2 tsp pepper, or to taste
4 cloves garlic, minced
1 cup roughly diced bell peppers
2 cups roughly chopped green cabbage
1/2 cup water
1/4 cup coconut sauce
5-6 mushrooms, thickly sliced
2 cups roughly chopped spinach
8-10 cherry tomatoes

I almost did not create this recipe. I had it in my head that you could not have egg rolls without that little packet of sauce, but that sauce is super high in sugars and starches.

To most people, walking away from a dish would not be a problem; for me, it became a challenge. This meant "how can I make egg rolls work?" was dancing in my head every time I rolled over in my sleep, night after night.

Leaning on the memory of how egg roll fillings taste, and a sprinkling of how I wanted this new dish to be without the sauce, I set out to make it happen.

There is no hint of plum sauce in this recipe, but there is loads of flavour.

Geoff likes his with hot sauce, while I like to top mine with a sunny-side-down egg. Just make a sunny-side-up egg and flip it upside down on your egg roll in a bowl.

1. Place the oil in a large sauté pan on a medium-high heat. When the oil is hot, add the onion and cook until it starts to turn translucent, about 2 to 3 minutes. Add the meat and spices, and with a wooden spoon break up the beef as it browns. Add the garlic and cook for 5 minutes.
2. If using any of the flavour variations on page 166, add the spices directly to the oil to help the spices bloom.
3. Add the peppers and cook for 3 to 5 minutes or until they begin to soften. Add the cabbage, water, and coconut sauce. Cover to steam the cabbage until it is wilted, stirring occasionally so that it is mixed through and cooks evenly. Add the mushrooms and cook 2 to 3 minutes, then add the spinach and tomatoes, mix well, and cook for 5 to 10 minutes. Adjust the liquid level, adding extra water for a sauce in the pan.

NOTE: Add extra water to the pan when sautéing the cabbage to help steam it. Serve with a sunny-side-up egg on the top.

❖ **VARIATIONS**

The best part of this recipe is swapping out these ingredients for different flavour sets. In our home, we call the recipe above Vanilla Egg Roll. It is not literally vanilla-flavoured; it is the plain version on which many different variations are built. Travel around the world with these spice variations. Add the following spice combos to the vanilla recipe.

Morocco flavour
1 tsp ground cardamom
1 tsp curry powder
1/2 tsp chili powder
1/2 tsp cloves
1/8 tsp Ceylon cinnamon
1/8 tsp nutmeg

Barcelona flavour
1 1/2 tsp chili powder
1 tsp ground cumin
1 tsp garlic powder
1/2 tsp onion powder
1/4 tsp dried oregano
1/4 tsp smoked paprika

New Orleans flavour
1 tbsp garlic powder
1 1/2 tsp onion powder
1 tsp smoked paprika
1 tsp cayenne pepper
1 1/2 tsp dried oregano
1/4 tsp dried thyme

Tuscany flavour
2 tsp garlic powder
1 tsp dried oregano
1 tsp dried parsley
1/2 tsp onion powder
1/2 tsp dried thyme
1/2 tsp dried basil
1/4 tsp dried sage
1/4 tsp Korean chili flakes (optional)

Alberta BBQ flavour
1 tsp ground cumin
1 tsp smoked paprika
1 tsp garlic powder
1 tsp onion powder
1 tsp chili powder
1 tsp powdered sweetener
1/4 tsp Korean chili flakes (optional)

Mumbai flavour
1 tsp ground coriander
1 tsp ground cumin
1 tsp turmeric
1/2 tsp ground cardamom
1/2 tsp ground ginger
1/8 tsp mustard powder
pinch of cinnamon
pinch of cayenne pepper

Cancun flavour
1 tsp chili powder
1 tsp garlic powder
1/2 tsp onion powder
1/2 tsp dried oregano
1 tsp smoked paprika
1/2 tsp ground cumin
1/4 tsp Korean chili flakes (optional)
pinch of Ceylon cinnamon
pinch of cloves

Montego Bay flavour
2 tsp garlic powder
1 tsp powdered sweetener
1 tsp cayenne pepper (optional)
1/2 tsp onion powder
1/2 tsp allspice
1/4 tsp dried thyme
1/4 tsp mustard powder
1/8 tsp nutmeg
pinch of cloves

MEAT ENTRÉES | 167

Grilled Spatchcock Chicken
WITH MAPLE GARLIC AND CINCO DE MAYO BBQ SAUCES

▶ **EXTRA: CINQO DE MAYO BBQ SAUCE / MAPLE GARLIC SAUCE**

1 whole chicken
oil, to drizzle
2 tsp salt
1 tsp pepper

Spatchcocking a chicken results in crispier skin and shorter cooking time than cooking a full chicken, especially if grilling. It also allows the meat to stay on the bone, which means juicier meat.

The term *spatchcock* is debated in the culinary world. It involves removing the chicken backbone and cracking the chicken in order to lay it flat like a book. It allows full contact with the grill and even overall cooking. My foodie friends in the UK and Australia would argue that a spatchcock is a young chicken. Taking this into account, maybe we could spatchcock (verb) a spatchcock (noun) using this recipe.

Spatchcock chicken can be cooked in the oven or in an air fryer, or grilled over indirect heat.

To oven-roast
1. Preheat the oven to 375°F.
2. On a cutting board with breasts facing down and the spine of the chicken facing up, cut out both sides of the backbone with kitchen shears. Discard the bone. Spread open the cavity and flip the chicken over so that the uncut skin side of the chicken faces up. Place your hands in the centre of the chicken breasts and press down until the wishbone cracks. Then the chicken can be totally flattened.
3. Drizzle the chicken skin with the oil and season with salt and pepper. Roast on a rack that has been placed on a baking sheet until the skin is crisp and the thickest part of the breast reaches an internal temperature of 165°F, about 35 minutes.
4. Let stand for 5 minutes before cutting the chicken in pieces.

To grill
1. If cooking the chicken on a grill, turn on one side of the BBQ and close the cover. You need to know your grill and learn what setting will give you the temperature you want given the wind and weather conditions. You want a temperature of about 300°F. A remote temperature probe will help.
2. When the BBQ has reached the correct temperature, place the chicken skin side up on the side of the grill that is not heated. As the grill is being used as an oven, the chicken should not be placed over the direct heat source. Close the cover and continue to monitor the temperature. The chicken is ready when the skin is crisp and the thickest part of the breast reads 165°F on a thermometer, about 35 minutes. Let stand for 5 minutes before cutting the chicken into pieces.

NOTE: If using sauce, add it in the final one-third of the cooking time; if it is added before this, it will burn before the chicken is cooked. If using an air fryer, follow the oven method and reduce the temperature by 25°F.

Spice it up with any spice combinations, such as those on page 166, or use these sauces to enhance the chicken's flavour.

170 | MEAT ENTRÉES

► CINQO DE MAYO BBQ SAUCE

A Mexican-inspired grill sauce with a delicate spice. Spiced but not spicy.

4 tbsp oil	1 tsp paprika
1 medium onion, minced	1 1/2 tsp ground cumin
2 cloves garlic, minced	1 tsp ground coriander
3/4 cup powdered sweetener	1 tsp chili powder
2 cups tomato sauce	1 tsp dried sage
2/3 cup tequila, 100% blue agave only (replace with broth for a non-alcoholic version)	1 1/2 tsp dried parsley
	1 tsp salt
	1/2 tsp pepper
1/3 cup apple cider or white vinegar	pinch of nutmeg
1 tsp dried oregano	1 tsp mustard powder

► MAPLE GARLIC SAUCE

This sweet and savoury sauce can be mixed in a bowl and added to the meat as it cooks, or cook in advance in a saucepan for maximum caramelization.

3 tbsp olive oil	1 tbsp paprika
1 shallot, minced	2 tsp ground coriander
4 cloves garlic, minced	1 tsp dried tarragon
1 1/2 cups tomato sauce	1 tsp garlic powder
2 tbsp coconut sauce	1 tsp salt
1/2 cup apple cider vinegar	1/2 tsp pepper
1/2 cup Maple Syrup Substitute (page 283)	1/2 tsp dried thyme
1 cup water	1/2 tsp Korean chili flakes

Sauté the onion and/or garlic in the oil for 3 minutes, then add the remaining ingredients. Whisk all the ingredients together and cook at a low temperature, stirring often. Reduce until it has reached the desired thickness.

NOTE: Sprinkle in xanthan gum to thicken if needed.

Honey-ish Balsamic Pork Chops

1 tbsp oil

4 pork chops

1 tsp salt

1 tsp garlic powder

1 tsp dried oregano

1/2 tsp pepper

1/2 tsp each of dried thyme, parsley, and basil

FOR THE HONEY-ISH BALSAMIC SAUCE

2 tbsp butter

2 green onions, chopped (reserve greens)

4 garlic cloves, minced

1 tsp fresh thyme

1 tsp salt

1 tsp Korean chili flakes

1/2 tsp pepper

1/4 cup white balsamic vinegar

1/4 cup powdered sweetener

1/2 cup water

2 tbsp Dijon mustard

1/8 tsp xanthan gum (optional)

TO FINISH THE SAUCE

1/4 cup white balsamic vinegar

2 tsp dried oregano

1 tsp each of dried garlic, thyme, basil, and parsley

3 tbsp whipping cream

green onion or parsley, for garnish

I wanted to call this recipe "Ish Pork Chops" because these chops taste like honey and balsamic even though the recipe uses neither of those ingredients in a traditional sense. But I'm sure it would leave many wondering what an Ish was and how you cook it. I was also pretty certain I wouldn't get that title past the editor of this lovely cookbook.

Avoid dark balsamic vinegar, as the dark colour is burnt sugar; opt for white balsamic vinegar instead. It has all the taste of the darker cousin, but nowhere near the blood glucose spike/carb count. Honey is also high in natural sugar; instead, use a sweetener that has a lower glycemic index rating. These substitutions do not affect the taste of the dish.

Finish the sauce with an Italian flair to bring out the flavours of the balsamic even more. The roasted veggies from page 108 are the perfect accompaniment to these chops.

To prepare the pork chops
1. Preheat the oven to 375°F.
2. Combine the seasonings and use them to coat the pork chops.
3. Place the oil in a large oven-safe sauté pan or Dutch oven on a medium-high heat. When the oil is hot, add the seasoned pork chops and sear on each side for 3 minutes. Remove them from the pan and set aside.

To prepare the honey-ish balsamic sauce
To the same pan, add the butter, onion, garlic, and spices. Cook for 2 minutes on a medium heat. Add the vinegar to deglaze the pan, taking care to scrape all the tasty brown bits off the bottom. Add the sweetener, water, and mustard and stir while continuing to cook.

To assemble
Nestle the pork chops in the sauce in the pan and spoon the sauce all over the chops. Transfer the pan to the oven to finish cooking: 15 to 20 minutes, or until the internal temperature of the chops reaches 145°F. Remove the pork chops from the sauce and set aside to rest.

To finish the sauce
1. Place the empty pork chop pan on the burner on a medium heat and add the vinegar and extra seasonings. Sprinkle the optional xanthan gum into the sauce (before it goes in the oven) to thicken the sauce as an alternative to reducing it.
2. Cook, while stirring, until the sauce reaches the desired thickness. Turn off the heat and stir in the cream. Sprinkle the reserved green onions or parsley on the chops.

NOTE: This sauce can be made in a separate saucepan and then poured over the pork chops.

Lemon Chicken

1 1/2 lb boneless, skinless chicken breasts, cut in 2-inch pieces
1 large egg, lightly beaten

FOR THE DREDGE
1/2 cup almond flour
1 tsp salt
1/2 tsp pepper
1/2 tsp garlic powder
zest of 1 lemon

FOR THE LEMON SAUCE
2 tbsp oil
3 cloves garlic, minced and then mashed
2 tsp grated fresh ginger
1 cup chicken broth or water
2 tbsp coconut sauce
juice of 2 lemons
zest of 1 lemon
1/4 cup powdered sweetener
1/8 tsp xanthan gum (optional)

FOR GARNISH
1 tsp sesame seeds
thinly sliced green onions
lemon slices

Lemon Chicken is not often found on a buffet line but it can be found in some à la carte selections. This, along with egg-fried faux rice, sweet and sour pork, and honey garlic ribs, has become a star of my Asian theme nights. The sauce is not as yellow as the restaurant sauce, which is usually achieved by yellow food colouring. Avoid such dyes.

For a more intense lemon flavour, add a few drops of food-grade lemon oil or extract.

To prepare the lemon sauce
Heat the oil in a large saucepan on a medium-high heat. Add the garlic and ginger and cook for about 45 to 60 seconds, then add the remaining sauce ingredients. Whisk and bring to a boil until the sweetener dissolves, then reduce the heat to a simmer and continue to cook.

To prepare the chicken
1. Place the dredge ingredients in a pie plate or a flat-bottomed bowl and whisk to incorporate.
2. Use a fork to place the chicken pieces in the dredge, one by one, and then use a spoon to press the dredge onto the chicken pieces. Set the coated chicken aside and continue coating the other pieces.
3. In a wok (filled to about one-third of its capacity) or a deep fryer, heat the oil to 325°F and cook the chicken pieces in batches for about 3 minutes or until golden and cooked through. Place the cooked chicken pieces on paper towel to blot any excess oil. When all the chicken has been cooked, reheat the sauce if it has cooled. If the sauce has not thickened enough, whisk in about 1/8 teaspoon xanthan gum before adding the chicken. Heat the sauce for another 30 seconds or until it has thickened slightly, then add the chicken pieces and toss to coat.
4. Transfer to a serving plate and add garnish, if using.
5. Serve with roasted vegetables (page 108).

✔ **TIP**
Try this sauce with the orange spices (page 34) instead of the lemon spices in this recipe.

MEAT ENTRÉES | 175

Masala-Spiced Pork Chops

6 pork chops
1 cup chicken broth
1 medium onion, chopped
6 cloves garlic
2 tsp grated fresh ginger
1 1/2 tsp salt
2 tsp garam masala
1 tsp fennel seed, ground with a mortar and pestle
1/2 tsp chili powder
1/2 tsp dried thyme
1/2 tsp pepper
1/2 tsp curry powder
1 tsp smoked paprika
1/4 tsp ground cumin
1/4 tsp ground coriander

Geoff and I both love to cook. Whether it's time alone in the kitchen or both of us playing side by side, there's always a sense of enjoyment, creativity, and relaxation.

Geoff usually takes the traditional route, following our own recipes for meals like Jiggs' dinners or burgers. He is the maintainer of normalcy.

Me, on the other hand, I'm the baby goat of the family. I never make the same meal twice and I won't even follow my own recipes. Gotta tweak and explore and make them a little better and different, each time. To methodical people like Geoff, I am chaos on wheels.

I can usually define what I'm eating, easily picking out the flavour profiles and spices used in a dish. Which is why this meal was such a pleasant surprise. It was Geoff's night to cook and when I saw pork chops, I knew they would be good. But when I tasted the dish, I was stumped. It was perfectly balanced and spiced, but I could not pinpoint the main flavour.

Geoff loosely based his dish on our paprika pork chops recipe. He played with the flavour profile and created a masala-spiced masterpiece.

1. Blot the pork chops on a paper towel.
2. Preheat the oven to 375°F.
3. Place the pork chops side by side in a braising or oven-safe dish with a tightly fitting lid. Do not stack the pork chops on top of each other. Add the broth. It should come only about halfway up the sides of the pork chops. Add the onion, garlic, and ginger.
4. Mix the dry ingredients in a small bowl, sprinkle on the pork chops, then cover and transfer the dish to the oven. Bake for 90 minutes (or until the pork reaches an internal temperature of 145°F), turning halfway.
5. Remove the pork chops to a plate and reduce the sauce while they rest.
6. Pour the reduced pan juices over the pork chops on the plate.

Mongolian Beef

FOR THE MARINADE

1/8 cup coconut sauce
1/8 cup powdered sweetener
1/4 cup water
1 tsp finely grated fresh ginger
4 cloves garlic, minced then pulverized
1/2 tsp Korean chili flakes
3 tbsp oil
1 medium onion, roughly chopped
1 lb flank, top sirloin, or round steak, sliced 1/4 inch thick across the grain

sliced green onions, for garnish

OPTIONAL VEGETABLES

1/2 bell pepper, sliced
6 mushrooms, sliced
1 cup sliced broccoli florets

Any cut of beef can be used for this rich and satisfying dish, but the tenderness of the final dish will depend on the tenderness of the cut. Cooking at a low temperature and for a long time is key to helping to keep this dish tender. Feel free to let it cook even longer than the recipe says: just be mindful of the liquid level and top up with water and/or broth as needed.

Serve Mongolian Beef with a side serving of sautéed or roasted vegetables, or just go with the optional veggies and turn this tasty dish into a full meal.

1. Place the marinade ingredients in a medium glass bowl or a large freezer bag. Add the sliced steak, toss to coat evenly, and let sit for 10 minutes while preparing the vegetables.
2. Preheat the oven to 300°F.
3. Heat a large oven-safe sauté pan on a high heat and add the oil. Add the steak in a single layer. Work in batches to avoid overcrowding the pan. Cook on each side for about 1 minute or until the edges start to brown. When the steak is cooked, set it aside on a plate. Repeat the process with the remaining steak.
4. Reduce the heat to medium. Add the onion and cook for about 3 minutes or until the onion turns translucent. Add the optional vegetables and cook for 2 to 3 more minutes. Add any remaining marinade to the pan and cook for 2 to 3 minutes. Add the steak and mix it into the sauce and vegetables, then transfer the pan to the preheated oven and bake for 45 minutes to 1 hour.
5. Garnish with the chopped green onions.

NOTE: If the pieces are too close together when browning, the juices that are released from the cooking steak will result in tough boiled steak. Use a glass bowl when marinating meats as the marinade can react with a metal or plastic bowl.

OMJ Half-Baked Chicken

2 tsp smoked paprika
2 tsp garlic powder
2 tsp ground ginger
1 tsp garam masala
1 tsp ground cardamom
1 tsp turmeric
1 tsp ground coriander
1 tsp salt
1/2 tsp dried parsley
1/2 tsp pepper
1/4 tsp nutmeg
4 boneless, skinless chicken breasts
2 tbsp oil

FOR THE SAUCE

juice from 1 can (28 oz) whole tomatoes
    (reserve the whole tomatoes)
1/2 cup apple cider vinegar
1/2 cup powdered sweetener
1 tsp salt
1 tsp garlic powder
1 tsp dried thyme
1 tsp Korean chili flakes
reserved whole tomatoes

FOR THE GARNISH

1 tsp dried parsley, or a few sprigs
    of fresh parsley, chopped

When I'm at the wheel, dinner just happens in our house. I throw stuff in the pan all willy-nilly, with no plan or recipe involved. I often get asked how my recipes come into being, or what's my process. Other than healthifying my own family recipes, the answer would be this (see above!)

It used to drive Geoff bonkers that I could have a dozen different pans going with no plan. It seemed like total chaos but somehow every time the end results were Ohhh My Jumpins good. That's exactly how OMJ Half-Baked Chicken happened!

Make sure to use whole tomatoes for this recipe. We keep them whole and gently warm them at the end of the cooking time. They will almost taste like warm fresh tomatoes from a sunlit garden.

1. Preheat the oven to 350°F.
2. Mix the spices in a small mixing bowl.
3. Lay the chicken breasts on a piece of waxed paper or aluminum foil, then sprinkle half the spice mixture on each chicken breast.
4. Put the oil in a large oven-safe sauté pan on a medium-high heat. When the oil is hot, place the breasts in the pan, seasoned side down, and cook for 4 to 5 minutes. While the chicken is cooking, sprinkle the unseasoned side with the spice mixture, then continue making the sauce.
5. Pour the tomato liquid only (do not add the tomatoes yet) into another medium saucepan. Add the spices and sweetener and continue to cook on a medium heat for the whole time that the chicken is on the stovetop.
6. Add the vinegar to the pan with the chicken now to deglaze the pan. Use a mini spatula to scrape the tasty bits off the sides and down into the sauce!
8. Flip the chicken and cook for another 4 to 5 minutes and then turn off the heat, keeping the chicken in the pan.
9. Place the cooked sauce in with the chicken, taking care to totally cover the chicken pieces.
10. Add the reserved whole tomatoes to the pan and cozy them in, around the chicken pieces, and garnish with a flourish of parsley.
11. Roast uncovered, for 20 minutes, or until the internal temperature of the thickest part of the chicken breasts reaches 165°F.
12. Set aside to cool for 5 minutes before removing carefully from the pan.

✔ **TIP**

When adding spices, especially as a garnish, place your hand at least 1 foot above the pan/dish. Sprinkle high and wide, and let it rain spices, while keeping an eye on where the spices are falling. This places the spices evenly over the top of the dish. When broiling, we use a wooden spoon propped/stuck in at the top to keep the door from fully closing. This keeps the oven on full force during the broiling time, instead of cutting back when it reaches the set temperature. Don't step away while broiling.

Pork Chops
WITH MUSHROOM RAGOUT

1 tbsp oil
2 lb bone-in or boneless pork chops
1 tsp paprika
1 tsp salt
1/2 tsp pepper
8 oz mushrooms, sliced
5 cloves garlic, whole
1 tbsp Dijon mustard
2 tsp sunflower lecithin (optional)
1/4 tsp xanthan gum
2 cups beef broth
1/4 cup whipping cream
1/2 cup sour cream

It was an easy comfort meal of the past: put pork chops in a pan, dump in a can of mushroom soup and some water, and flick the switch to bake. Easy, right?

These days we're trying to do better. We know those canned soups are also full of preservatives and other items that aren't so good for our health ... but we still want easy.

Ta-da! This recipe fits the bill. It tastes even better than the original recipe! And you get the satisfaction of knowing you've fed your family a healthy meal that everybody will love.

1. Preheat the oven to 350°F. Season both sides of the pork chops with the salt and pepper. Add 1 teaspoon garlic powder for an intense garlic flavour.
2. Put the oil in an oven-safe sauté pan on a medium-high heat. When the oil is hot, add the pork chops and sear for about 2 to 3 minutes on each side until browned. Transfer to a plate and set aside.
3. Add the remaining ingredients—except the broth, cream, and sour cream—to the pan, and sauté for about 2 more minutes. Stir in the broth, cream, and sour cream. Turn off the stovetop and return the pork chops to the pan. Spoon some of the liquid on the chops to cover them. Roast for 60 to 75 minutes, until cooked through and the sauce has thickened. Check several times while roasting and spoon pan liquid on the chops. When the chops are tender, spoon the mushroom sauce from the pan on them, and garnish with additional pepper, Parmesan cheese, and fresh herbs.

NOTE: The xanthan gum and sunflower lecithin may be whisked together before being whisked into the wet ingredients.

Did you know?
Sunflower lecithin is an emulsifier that stabilizes mixtures and prevents separation. Lecithin is a fatty substance naturally found in the human body and in foods such as eggs and sunflower seeds. Soy lecithin should be avoided.

MEAT ENTRÉES | 183

Pork Chops
WITH IRISH WHISKEY SAUCE

1 tsp dried oregano
1 tsp garlic powder
1/2 tsp dried basil
1/2 tsp dried parsley
1/2 tsp dried thyme
1/2 tsp paprika
1/2 tsp onion powder
1/4 tsp dried rosemary
1 tsp salt
1/2 tsp pepper
1 lb boneless pork chops
2 tbsp oil
1 medium onion, thickly sliced
6-8 mushrooms
3 cloves garlic, minced

FOR THE WHISKEY SAUCE
1 tbsp butter
1 tbsp coconut flour
1 oz cream cheese
1/3 cup Irish whiskey
2/3 cup chicken or vegetable broth
1/2 cup whipping cream
2 tbsp coconut sauce
2 tsp nutritional yeast
1 tsp dried oregano
1 tsp salt
1/4 tsp dried basil
1/3 tsp dried parsley
1/4 tsp dried thyme
1/4 tsp pepper

fresh parsley, for garnish

In Ireland, this word is spelled *whiskey*; in Scotland, it is *whisky*. Rumour has it that in the 1800s Scottish whisky was cheaply put together and the Irish producers wanted to distance themselves from this Scottish version, so they changed the spelling of their own product.

If you prefer an alcohol-free dish, note that at no point does the cooking process remove all traces of alcohol. Baking or simmering an alcohol-containing dish for 2 1/2 hours will still leave 5 per cent of the alcohol content behind. According to the US Department of Agriculture, baked or simmered dishes that contain alcohol will retain 40 per cent of the original amount after 15 minutes of cooking, 35 per cent after 30 minutes, and 25 per cent after 1 hour. The greater the surface area, the greater the exposure of the alcohol to the air, and the faster the alcohol content will be released. Based on this, it is assumed there will be less alcohol in a dish simmered in a wide-based pan than one simmered in a small saucepan.

The only way to ensure an alcohol-free dish is to avoid adding alcohol at any stage. In this recipe, substitute broth for the whiskey, if desired.

To prepare the pork chops
1. Prepare a dry rub with the spices and coat the pork chops with it at least 1/2 hour before cooking.
2. Heat the oil in an oven-safe large sauté pan on a medium-high heat. When the oil is hot, add the pork chops and onion and sear the chops for 4 to 5 minutes per side, for a total of 8 to 10 minutes. Remove the pork chops and transfer to a plate.
3. Add the mushrooms and garlic to the pan and cook for 5 to 6 minutes on a medium heat. Add them to the plate with the pork chops.
4. Preheat the oven to 375°F.

To prepare the whiskey sauce
1. Place the butter in the sauté pan on a medium heat and stir in the coconut flour. Cook for about 1 minute, whisking the flour into the butter. When the two are well incorporated, stir in the whiskey and cook for 5 to 10 minutes. Add the beef broth, coconut sauce, spices, and cream and simmer for 2 to 3 minutes.
2. Return the pork chops and mushrooms to the sauté pan with the sauce. Add water to ensure that the pork chops are three-quarters immersed. Transfer the pan to the oven for 15 to 20 minutes or until the chops reach an internal temperature of 145°F. Remove from the oven and sprinkle with chopped parsley. Serve immediately.

Red Pepper Meatloaf

1 lb ground beef
1/2 lb ground pork
1 large egg
1 medium onion, diced
2 cloves garlic, finely chopped
1 red pepper, finely diced
5 large white mushrooms, diced
1 tsp dried parsley
1 tsp salt
1 tsp Korean chili flakes
1 tsp paprika
1 tsp dried oregano
1/2 tsp pepper

FOR THE SAUCE

1 1/2 cups tomato sauce
1 tsp salt
1 tsp garlic powder
1 tsp paprika
1 tsp dried parsley
1/2 tsp dried sage

The flavour profile for this recipe came from one of our dog food recipes. We home-cook for our three dogs. Healthy eating is a family affair for us. I can't imagine nourishing the humans of our family with top-notch food and not giving our darling fur babies that same level of nourishment.

After creating and taste-testing (yes, we try them all!) this particular dog recipe, we were intrigued by the flavour. And so this meatloaf recipe was born. Without the onion, this recipe is pooch-friendly.

1. Line a lipped baking sheet with parchment paper and preheat the oven to 350°F.
2. Gently and thoroughly mix the meatloaf ingredients in a large mixing bowl by hand. Do not overmix, as this toughens the meat. Form into a loaf and set it on the prepared pan. Bake for 30 minutes, then remove the meatloaf from the oven.
3. While the meatloaf is cooking, mix the sauce ingredients together. Spoon the prepared sauce on the meatloaf and bake for another 20 to 30 minutes or until thoroughly cooked in the centre.
4. Place the meatloaf on a cutting board and place the pan drippings in a medium saucepan. Reduce to the desired consistency.
5. Cut the meatloaf in 1-inch-thick pieces and drizzle sauce on each serving.

NOTE: Add extra tomato sauce to stretch the sauce. This meatloaf can be baked in a loaf pan as well.

Roasted-Garlic-and-Parm-Crusted Pork

FOR THE ROASTED GARLIC CRUST
2 heads of garlic, separated into cloves
1 tbsp oil
water to cover the bottom of the pan
6 oz grated Parmesan cheese
2 tbsp oil
2 tsp dried parsley
1 tsp pepper

FOR THE PORK
2 tbsp oil
6 thick-cut, boneless pork loin chops
1 tsp salt
1 tsp paprika
1/2 tsp pepper
1 medium onion, roughly chopped
1 cup broth or water

If you've never roasted garlic, what are you waiting for? Roasting changes the chemical makeup of garlic so that it is much milder and tastes sweeter. When you cut, crush, or chew garlic, cell breakdown occurs in the sulphur compounds found in all alliums. These phytochemicals, in particular a compound called allicin, are mostly responsible for the sharp or hot taste and the strong smell of garlic. Cooking garlic removes allicin, mellowing its spiciness.

Eat caramelized roasted garlic cloves directly out of the heads, add them to faux pasta dishes, mash them with butter and spread them over toast, or mix them with sour cream for a dip.

To prepare the roasted garlic crust
1. Line a pan with parchment paper and preheat the oven to 350°F.
2. Separate the garlic into individual cloves and place them on the prepared tray. Drizzle the oil on the garlic and then add a thin layer of water to the bottom of the tray. Braise the cloves until the cloves split open and the insides are soft and caramelized, about 35 to 40 minutes, depending on the size of the cloves. Set aside to cool. When the cloves have cooled, remove the skins and any hard portions. Place the garlic in a small mixing bowl and mash. Add the remaining paste ingredients and stir well. Set aside.

To prepare the pork
1. Preheat the oven to 350°F.
2. Put the oil in a large braising pan on a high heat. Season the pork chops with the salt, pepper, and paprika. When the oil is hot, add the pork chops, taking care not to overcrowd the pan. Work in batches if needed and keep at least 1 inch between the chops. Sear them to a deep brown on both sides, then turn off the heat.
3. Add the onion and broth to the pan, ensuring that the liquid comes only about one-third of the way up the side of the chops. Bake, covered, for 1 hour. Flip the chops, check the liquid level, and bake until they are fork-tender, about 1 hour. Spoon the garlic paste on the chops, ensuring that the top is covered in a thick layer of paste. Set the oven to broil.
4. Broil until the garlic paste is slightly crisp. Remove when the crust has started to brown slightly. Allow the chops to rest in their juices for about 5 minutes. Transfer them to plates and spoon pan juices on the top.

NOTE: Brush oil on each garlic clove to ensure that it is fully coated. Before roasting whole heads of garlic, cut off the top portion first. Maintain the oven temperature at 350°F or less to ensure that the garlic does not scorch.

Storing roasted garlic
Refrigerate in an airtight container or freezer bag for up to 3 days. Submerge the garlic in olive oil and refrigerate for up to 1 week. Freeze the roasted garlic cloves on a baking sheet, then transfer the individually frozen cloves to a freezer bag. Freeze for up to 3 months.

Seared Duck Breast WITH CHERRY GASTRIQUE

❖ **VARIATION: DUCK WITH BLACKBERRY GRILL SAUCE**

2 large duck breasts, at room temperature
1 tsp salt
½ tsp pepper

FOR THE CHERRY GASTRIQUE

1/2 cup broth
1/2 cup red wine
1/2 cup water
1/2 cup white balsamic vinegar
2 tbsp Dijon mustard
2 tbsp powdered sweetener
3 sprigs of fresh thyme, or 1 tsp dried thyme
1/4 tsp cloves or nutmeg
1/2 cup pitted, sliced red cherries
1 tsp salt
1/2 tsp ground ginger
1/2 tsp pepper

TO FINISH

2 tbsp butter
sprigs of fresh thyme

It took us a few attempts to get duck down pat. Geoff and I often joke that not a lot of bad meals come out of our house. Undercooked fish was one of those and the other was duck breast. Both were an epic fail.

We persevered. We chatted with our chef friends and picked their brains. The result is a combination of all the solid advice we received, rolled into one doozie of a recipe. The top takeaway tip is to start with a cold pan so that the fat under the skin renders out slowly.

1. Preheat the oven to 400°F.
2. Blot the duck breasts with a paper towel, score the skin, taking care not to cut into the meat, and then season with salt and pepper.
3. Place the duck breasts skin side down in a cold oven-safe sauté pan and slowly heat it, pressing each down gently to ensure that all the skin comes in contact with the pan. Sauté until the skin is crispy and most of the fat is rendered out, usually about 6 to 8 minutes, depending on the size of the breasts. Flip the breasts to skin side up and turn off the heat.
4. Transfer the sauté pan to the preheated oven for 5 to 6 minutes, or until the breasts are medium rare, at 125°F. Do not let the temperature go above 130°F or the duck will dry out and be tough. The duck will continue to cook while it is resting. Transfer the breasts to a board or a plate and let them rest for 10 minutes. Do not tent, as this creates a mini oven and the duck will be overcooked. Allow it to slightly cool as it rests.

To prepare the cherry gastrique

1. While the duck is resting, drain (and reserve) half the fat.
2. Return the sauté pan to a medium heat and add the liquids to deglaze the pan, scraping up the browned bits from the bottom. Cook until the liquid is reduced by half. Add the remaining ingredients, reduce the heat to low, and simmer, stirring periodically, until the sauce sticks to the back of a spoon. Remove from the heat, whisk in the butter, and adjust the seasoning if needed.
3. Slice the duck into thick slices across the grain of the meat.
4. Fan the breast out, skin side up, on serving dishes, then drizzle with the balsamic sauce.
5. Garnish with fresh thyme leaves and serve immediately.

NOTE: There are many theories on how long to rest meats. Some say 5 minutes for every 1 inch (thickness) and others say to rest for half the cooking time. Remember that if a piece of cooked meat is cut into too soon, the liquids—and most of the flavour—will drain out on the cutting board. Let the meat sit uncovered while finishing side dishes, then cut just before serving.

❖ **VARIATION: DUCK BREAST WITH BLACKBERRY GRILL SAUCE**
Make as described above but deglaze with 1/2 cup Blackberry Grill Sauce (page 273) instead of the balsamic cherry sauce. Reduce and serve.

Shepherd's Pie

FOR THE FILLING

2 tbsp oil

1 carrot, diced

1 medium onion, chopped

2 lb ground beef, pork, or lamb

1 tbsp coconut sauce

2 tbsp dried parsley

1 tbsp paprika

1 tsp salt

1 tsp dried thyme

1/2 tsp pepper

2 cloves garlic, minced

1 tbsp coconut flour

1/2 cup dry red wine

FOR THE TOPPING

1 1/2 cups water

1/4 cup whipping cream

1 tsp salt

1 large celeriac, approximately
    2 cups peeled, cut in 1-inch cubes

4 cloves garlic, quartered

1 tbsp butter

1 oz cream cheese

1/4 tsp pepper

4 oz grated cheddar cheese (optional)

1 tbsp chopped fresh chives,
    thyme, or parsley

A traditional shepherd's pie is made with lamb, but this recipe offers an old-style dish in a different form.

The bones of this dish are a thick savoury stew, rustic vegetables, and a rich fragrant broth. You can use ground beef but also try ground lamb, stewing beef, cubed chicken, or even pork.

Shepherd's Pie is traditionally topped with a creamy mashed potato, but to achieve the exact effect with fewer carbs use mashed celeriac as a faux-tato layer to cover the top.

To prepare the filling
1. Place the oil, onion, and carrot in a large sauté pan on a medium heat; cook for about 3 to 5 minutes, then add the ground beef. Cook for about 5 minutes, breaking the beef into small pieces as it cooks. Add the coconut sauce and spices. Cook until the onion is translucent, about 5 minutes. Add the garlic and cook for 1 minute.
2. Whisk the coconut flour into the pan juices and allow it to cook for about 1 minute, then add the red wine. Cook until the sauce is reduced by about half and the lamb and vegetables are cooked through.
3. Turn off the heat and set aside to cool.

To prepare the topping
Bring the water and cream to a boil in a large saucepan on a medium-high heat. Add the salt, celeriac, and garlic and return to a boil. On a low-medium heat, simmer for 20 minutes or until the celeriac is tender. Drain well and place the celeriac in a blender. Add the butter and cream cheese and purée until smooth. Check the seasoning and add salt and pepper to taste. Set aside to slightly cool.

To assemble
1. Preheat the oven to 400°F.
2. Spoon the beef filling into an oven-safe casserole dish. Spread or pipe the celeriac purée on the beef filling and sprinkle with the cheese (if using) and herbs. Bake for 20 to 25 minutes, or until the cheese has melted.
3. Turn the broiler on high and broil for 2 to 4 minutes to brown the cheese, if desired.

✔ **TIP**
When peeling the celeriac, carefully dig out any cracks and crevices that could hide soil or dirt.

NOTE: Top with Irish Colcannon (page 108) instead of plain celeriac mash or scatter a layer of fresh herbs between the beef and faux-tato layers for extra flavour.

Slow-Roasted Maple Pork Loin
WITH SUN-DRIED TOMATOES AND MUSHROOMS

- 2–2 1/2 lb pork loin, seasoned with 2 tsp salt and 1 tsp pepper
- 2 tbsp oil
- 1/2 medium onion, peeled and roughly chopped
- 6 garlic cloves, whole, unpeeled
- 1/2 cup dry red wine, or 1/4 cup broth and 1/4 cup red wine vinegar
- 1 cup roughly sliced chanterelles, or any mushroom
- 1/4 cup diced sun-dried tomatoes
- 1/2 cup water or broth
- 1/4 cup Maple Syrup Substitute (page 283)
- 2 tbsp white balsamic vinegar
- 2 tbsp dried parsley
- 1 tsp ground ginger
- 1 tsp garlic powder
- 1 tsp salt
- 1/2 tsp garam masala
- 1/2 tsp pepper

This slow-cooked dish is perfect for a lazy Sunday when the whole family is at home relaxing. This is a set-it-and-forget-it recipe: put all the ingredients in the pan and spoon a little sauce over the meat every hour or so.

The maple syrup flavour marries with the red wine and creates a sticky and satisfying reduction.

1. Preheat the oven to 275°F.
2. Heat the oil in a large oven-safe sauté pan or Dutch oven on a medium heat. Add the pork and sear all sides until a deep golden-brown crust has formed. Add the remaining ingredients and roast for 4 to 5 hours, or until the pork is cooked throughout and fork-tender. Check hourly, adding water or broth as needed and basting the pork with the sauce each time. Remove the pork and vegetables to a serving platter to rest while making the sauce.
3. Add all the sauce ingredients to the same sauté pan and stir, on a medium-high heat, for 5 minutes or until it reduces. For a smooth sauce, strain to remove the bits of onions.
4. Slice the pork in thick slices and spoon or pour the thickened sauce on the top.
5. Serve the onions and mushrooms on the side.

NOTE: Pair this pork with Roasted Carrots with Carrot Top Chimichurri (page 120). Substitute broth and vinegar for the red wine for a non-alcoholic version if desired.

Stuffed Polpette al Sugo — Meatballs in Red Sauce

FOR THE POLPETTE
1/2 tsp ground cumin
1/2 tsp Ceylon cinnamon
1 tsp salt
1/2 tsp pepper
1 tsp dried parsley
1 tsp dried oregano
1/2 tsp fennel seeds, crushed
1/2 tsp dried rosemary
1/2 tsp dried thyme
1/2 tsp dried basil
2 tbsp yellow (or Dijon) mustard
3 oz grated Parmesan cheese
1 large egg
3 cloves garlic, minced
1 medium onion, diced
1 lb regular ground beef
1/2 lb ground pork
6 strips bacon, diced
1 oz buffalo mozzarella, per meatball
1/2 oz spicy salami, serrano ham, pepperoni, or chorizo, per meatball

FOR THE SUGO
2 tbsp oil
1/2 medium onion, minced
3 cloves garlic, minced
1 1/2 tsp dried oregano
1 tsp salt
1 tsp dried parsley
1 tsp garlic powder
1/2 tsp dried basil
1/2 tsp dried thyme
1/2 tsp pepper
2 cups tomato sauce or puréed canned tomatoes
1/2 cup red wine (optional)

These giant meatballs are delicately spiced with a centre of spicy meat and cheese. Polpette means eyelid in Italian. Maybe this culinary version was so named because the way the meatballs are prepared reminded someone of eyelids closing to protect the eyes.

Use any marinara or red sauce, but this traditional sugo is how it would have been made it in the old world.

Make sure you close the (meat) eyelids nice and tight so that the cheese doesn't seep out into the sauce.

To prepare the polpette
1. Combine all the spices in a small mixing bowl. Mix in the mustard, cheese, egg, and garlic. Add the garlic and onion. Set aside.
2. With a very light hand, mix the beef, pork, bacon, and mustard mixture. Form a patty with 2 to 3 tablespoons of the ground meat mixture.
3. Wrap half a slice of spicy salami around a small piece of mozzarella and place it on the patty.
4. Pinch the patty together, sealing the salami and mozzarella within the meatball. Roll to seal completely and place on a greased baking tray.
5. Repeat the process with the remaining meat mixture, salami, and mozzarella. Refrigerate the meatballs for at least 15 minutes.
6. While the meatballs are chilling, preheat the oven to 350°F and start the sauce.
7. Bake the meatballs for 20 to 25 minutes or until they reach an internal temperature of 165°F.

To prepare the sugo
Place the oil in a sauté pan on a medium-high heat. When the oil is hot, add the onion and sauté for 2 to 3 minutes. Add the garlic and continue to cook for 1 to 2 minutes. Add the herbs and spices to the oil, then whisk in the tomato and wine (if using). Reduce the heat to low and simmer for at least 15 minutes.

NOTE: Polpette can be baked, and then served with the sauce on the side, or baked as a complete casserole. To do so, spoon the sauce and 1/2 cup grated mozzarella cheese on the baked meatballs. Return to the oven and bake for 10 to 12 minutes at 375°F. Sprinkle Parmesan cheese and fresh parsley on the meatballs and serve with a Caesar salad or a green vegetable.

Desserts
The Main Attraction...

Addie's (Billy Miner) Cream Pie
Banana Cream Pie
Blissfully Cran-Bars
Blizzards
Blondies
Blueberry Cream Cake
Boston Cream Poke Cake
Chocolate Chip Cookie Skillet
Chocolate Faux Guinness Cake with Irish Whiskey Frosting
Cinnamon Coffee Cake Loaf
Cranberry Cheesecake with White Chocolate Mousse
Crustless Salted Caramel Cheesecake
Dark Chocolate Tart with Raspberry Coulis
Double Chocolate Peanut Butter Bars
Faux Apple Cake
French Vanilla Ice Cream
Ginger Crème Brûlée
Jamaican Rum Cake
Lilac Love Cake
Lime Chiffon Cake with Praline Crumb
Lisa and Brett's Nanaimo Cheesecake
Mixed Berry Crumble Squares
Peony and Pistachio Cake
Roly Poly
Shortbread Cookies
Sour Cream Glazed Donuts
Strawberry and Cream Mini Muffins
Strawberry Shortcake Deconstructed
Walnut Ginger Carrot Cake

In my grandparents' day, kids were excited to go trick or treating on Halloween to get treats—treats they didn't have access to the rest of the year. Christmas was a time to look forward to because every house had treats, sweets, and desserts. Food memories were created during these special times.

Today, sweets have become commonplace. We are over-consuming sweets and it's hurting our health. Our bodies were not meant to process so much of these foods.

As you journey toward health, reflect on the time when sweets were reserved for special occasions. Treat your sweet tooth with respect and think of sweets as something to reach for and look forward to. We have to relearn.

There is also a learning curve when you switch to a new way of eating and sweetener is probably the biggest lesson to learn.

First and foremost, check ingredients! No sense in starting a sugar-free health journey, only to use a replacement far more harmful to your body than sugar. Artificial (chemical) sweeteners such as aspartame and acesulfame potassium should be avoided. Watch for additives and fillers.

We recommend that you use a blender to powder any sweeteners as soon as you get them home. These food items don't react the same way that sugar does and, unfortunately, they all behave differently. For more info on sweeteners head over to our website before you buy.

Maybe our grandparents did know best after all: learn to limit sweets and, in turn, they will become more special.

Addie's (Billy Miner) Cream Pie
▶ EXTRA: CHOCOLATE DRIZZLE

1/2 pie crust recipe (page 56) with
   2 tbsp cocoa powder added
2 tbsp espresso powder or instant coffee
   granules, crushed
3/4 cup whipping cream
20 oz cream cheese, at room temperature
1 cup powdered sweetener
1 tsp pure vanilla extract
1/4 tsp salt

whipped cream sweetened with powdered
   sweetener, for garnish

unsweetened baking chocolate, for garnish

This recipe is for the young feller who always makes me laugh and holds a gigantic portion of my heart. Somewhere along the way, he also helped me to realize what true and pure love really means.

This is my version of the steakhouse coffee-flavoured pie that my kid absolutely devoured every time we ate out as a family. This dessert is best served super cold or even semi-frozen. It's delightfully refreshing on a warm summer day and is guaranteed to make all your people happy, not just the kids!

Alex, this was always your very favourite. I hope you make it often in your own life and think of Mom and home.

1. Blind-bake the pie crust according to the instructions on page 56 and refrigerate while making the coffee filling.
2. Dissolve the coffee in the cream, then add the remaining ingredients and combine with a mixer at a high speed until smooth and creamy. Pour into a cooled crust. Freeze for 1 hour or refrigerate for 3 hours to set.
3. Pipe or spread whipped cream on the edges and shave baking chocolate on the pie to garnish.

NOTE: This pie can also be made in a springform pan as a cheesecake. Freeze extras on a sheet tray in individual slices. When frozen, transfer the individual pieces, separating with a small piece of parchment paper, to a freezer bag. Microwave the chocolate for 10 to 15 seconds and use a vegetable peeler to make the chocolate curls.

▶ **EXTRA: CHOCOLATE DRIZZLE**
1/2 cup whipping cream
2 oz unsweetened baking chocolate, roughly chopped
1 oz butter
1/8 cup powdered sweetener

Heat the chocolate in a double boiler on a medium heat. Add the cream and sweetener and whisk until combined. Drizzle on the chilled pie. Freeze the pie for 1 hour or refrigerate for 3 hours, preferably overnight.

Banana Cream Pie

❖ **VARIATION: GRASSHOPPER PIE**

1 pie crust recipe (page 56)
8 oz cream cheese, at room temperature
1 cup whipping cream
1/2 cup powdered sweetener
1 large egg
2 large egg yolks
1 tsp pure vanilla extract
1 tsp banana extract
1/8 tsp xanthan gum
1/8 tsp salt
1 tbsp butter

sweetened whipped cream, for garnish

unsweetened baking chocolate shavings, for garnish (optional)

We've all heard that bananas are a really good source of potassium, but what is even more prevalent in bananas is sugar. The original fruit looked very different than the ones in our stores today—they were smaller, full of seeds, and nowhere near as sweet. Over the years, bananas have been cultivated to where they are hardly recognized as the same. In the pursuit of making a "better" banana, cultivators have made them so sweet that they are a hazard to our health. Bananas are a blood glucose spike waiting to happen. Remove or drastically reduce your intake of bananas if your goal is to reduce carbs/sugars.

In this recipe, we pull banana extract into action to get the banana taste in this custard pie.

Once you've mastered this version of custard pie, the sky is the limit.

1. Blind-bake the pie crust according to the instructions on page 56 and refrigerate while making the filling.
2. Mix the filling ingredients together in a saucepan on a low-medium heat. Allow to come to a gentle boil while stirring, then reduce the heat to a simmer. Simmer until the filling coats the back of a spoon, about 5 to 7 minutes. Remove from the heat and stir in the butter. Cool completely.
3. When both the crust and the filling have cooled, spoon the filling into the crust. Pipe or spread whipped cream around the edges and shave the baking chocolate on the pie to garnish.

✔ **TIP**
Slightly warm blocks of baking chocolate in the microwave for 10 to 15 seconds and then use a carrot peeler to make large chocolate swirls.

❖ **VARIATION: GRASSHOPPER PIE**
Instead of banana extract, add 2 tablespoons cocoa powder to the crust and 1/4 teaspoon peppermint extract and 3 to 4 drops natural green food colouring to the filling. Add 3 tablespoons cocoa powder to the whipped topping.

DESSERT | 203

DESSERT

Blissfully Cran-Bars

❖ **VARIATION: CRANBERRY ORANGE BISCOTTI**

FOR THE CRANBERRIES

1-1 1/2 cups fresh or frozen cranberries, quartered
1/2 cup powdered sweetener, or to taste
1/8 cup olive oil, or equivalent

FOR THE BARS

2 cups almond flour
1 cup powdered sweetener
2 tbsp coconut flour
1 tsp cream of tartar
1/2 tsp baking soda
1/4 tsp xanthan gum
1/8 tsp nutmeg
pinch of salt
1 tbsp butter
4 oz cream cheese
1/2 cup whipping cream
5 drops liquid stevia
1 tsp pure vanilla extract
1/4 tsp orange extract, or 2 drops orange food-grade oil
3 large eggs
1/3 cup dried cranberries, diced (prepared in the first step)

FOR THE FROSTING

6 oz cream cheese
1/4 cup powdered sweetener
pinch of salt
1/4 cup chopped dried cranberries, for garnish

In these Starbucks-inspired cranberry bars, the orange has been toned down. Orange can overpower some recipes rather quickly, and here the star of the show should be cranberry.

Add a hint of orange in the cream cheese icing, but creamy vanilla contrasts beautifully with the orange cranberry bars. For purists who love the orange notes in the original bars, add 1/2 teaspoon orange oil or 2 teaspoons orange extract to the batter.

Do not use commercially dried cranberries as they are loaded with sugar.

To prepare the cranberries

1. Line a baking sheet with parchment paper and preheat the oven to 170°F, or the lowest oven setting. If using a dehydrator, set it at 135°F and use the leather (solid) dehydrator tray for the first 2 hours to reduce spillage.
2. Combine all the ingredients and toss to combine.
3. Place the coated berries on the prepared pan and separate them as much as possible. Dry in the oven or dehydrator for 1 hour and stir them to ensure that all sides are covered in oil. Repeat at hour two.
4. After 2 1/2 hours, remove the tray and blot the excess oil. Return to the oven or dehydrator for at least another 1/2 hour.
5. Remove, when dehydrated, and let cool. Store in an airtight container.

To prepare the bars

1. Line an 8- by 11-inch baking pan with parchment paper. Preheat the oven to 350°F.
2. Mix the dry ingredients together, including the sweetener, in a large mixing bowl. Cream the butter into the dry mixture and then continue with the cream cheese. Add the eggs, liquid stevia, and vanilla. Fold in the cranberries. Bake for 25 to 35 minutes, until lightly browned on the top.
3. Set aside to cool.

To prepare the frosting

Cream the frosting ingredients together, spread on the cooled bars, and garnish with the cranberries. Refrigerate for at least 1/2 hour before cutting into bars.

NOTE: Use a larger pan for thinner bars.

❖ **VARIATION: CRANBERRY ORANGE BISCOTTI**

Trim off the edges and use them for biscotti. Place the cut slices on a parchment-paper-covered baking sheet. Bake in a preheated 350°F oven for 12 to 16 minutes. These crisp up fast.

Blizzards

FOR THE COATING

1 cup medium unsweetened coconut

2 tbsp powdered sweetener

FOR THE COOKIE

1 1/2 cups almond flour

8 oz cream cheese

1 cup flax meal

1 1/2 cups fine unsweetened coconut

3/4 cup butter

1 cup powdered sweetener

1 tbsp psyllium husk

1 tsp pure vanilla extract

pinch of salt

We all grew up eating snowballs, those chocolatey coconut balls that come around every Christmas. Every nan had her own version of the recipe and there were definitely some bragging rights to having the moistest snowballs at a church or community function.

This vanilla version is bound to be a nan-approved family favourite. Try these on the next stormy night.

1. Mix together the coating ingredients. Set aside.
2. Place the cookie ingredients in a medium saucepan and simmer on a low heat, stirring constantly. When the batter has come together and the ingredients have melted, refrigerate the saucepan for 30 minutes.
3. Use a mini ice cream scoop to form the batter into small balls. Roll the balls in the coating, pressing the coconut into the cookie. Refrigerate.

NOTE: If the coating is not sticking, add a little cream to the batter. Add 2 heaping tablespoons cocoa powder and 1 teaspoon espresso powder to the cookie mixture for more traditional chocolate snowballs.

Blondies

❖ **VARIATION: TRIPLE CHOCOLATE BROWNIES**

FOR THE BLONDIES
2 1/2 cups almond flour
1 cup powdered sweetener
1 tbsp egg white powder
1 tsp cream of tartar
1/2 tsp baking soda
1/2 tsp salt
1/4 tsp xanthan gum
1/2 cup butter, at room temperature
3 large eggs
3/4 cup whipping cream
1 tsp pure vanilla extract
1 tsp apple cider or white vinegar
2 oz White Chocolate, grated (page 295)

FOR THE ICING
8 oz cream cheese, at room temperature
4 oz butter, at room temperature
1/4 cup powdered sweetener, or to taste
1 tsp pure vanilla extract
1/4 tsp salt

This recipe made its public debut at the Unscripted Digital Arts festival in Twillingate, NL (September 2022), as a Creamy Vanilla Blondie with raspberry coulis and candied pecans. We paired it with a Triple Chocolate Brownie; both were dressed with a crumb and they were both absolutely divine.

It's always a pleasure for us to create our food for foodies who love trying new things, especially when we're cooking for people outside our own healthy/gluten-free community, and this event was no exception. These beautiful little bars were very well received.

1. Preheat the oven to 350°F and line a baking sheet with parchment paper.
2. In a large mixing bowl, combine all dry ingredients, including the sweetener. Cream in the butter, then whisk in the remaining ingredients. Pour the batter on the prepared baking sheet and bake for 20 to 25 minutes, turning at the midway mark.
3. Allow the blondies to cool before taking them out of the pan.
4. Combine the icing ingredients with a hand mixer and spread on the cooled blondies.

NOTE: These are best when served cold from the refrigerator. Try them with raspberry coulis (page 227).

❖ **VARIATION: TRIPLE CHOCOLATE BROWNIES**
Add 2 heaping tablespoons cocoa powder (1 dark and 1 regular), 1 teaspoon espresso powder, 2 ounces shaved unsweetened baking chocolate, and another teaspoon of vinegar to the batter, and bake as above. To the icing, add 2 tablespoons cocoa powder and 1/2 teaspoon espresso powder.

✔ **TIP**
Sprinkle 1 teaspoon pecan praline crumb (page 249) for an exquisite boost to these blondies.

Blueberry Cream Cake WITH STREUSEL TOPPING

FOR THE CREAM CHEESE FILLING

3/4 cup powdered sweetener
16 oz cream cheese, at room temperature
1 large egg
1/2 tsp pure vanilla extract

1 cup fresh blueberries

FOR THE CAKE

1 1/3 cups almond flour
1 cup powdered sweetener
1 tbsp egg white powder
1 tsp cream of tartar
1/2 tsp baking soda
1/4 tsp nutmeg
1/4 tsp xanthan gum
1/2 cup butter
2 large eggs
1 tsp pure vanilla extract
1/4 cup sour cream or whipping cream
5 drops liquid stevia, or to taste

FOR THE STREUSEL TOPPING

1/3 cup powdered sweetener
1/2 cup almond flour
3 tbsp butter, at room temperature

Vanilla cake on the bottom, blueberries and cheesecake in the middle, and blueberry streusel on the top: this is pure decadence. The amount of berries used reduces the natural sugar load (lowering the carb count), but they are strategically placed in order to have berries in every bite.

1. Mix all the cream cheese filling ingredients with a hand or stand mixer until fully incorporated and creamy. Set aside.
2. Preheat the oven to 350°F. Line the bottom and sides of a 9-inch springform pan with parchment paper. Set aside.
2. Mix all dry ingredients, including the sweetener, in a large mixing bowl. Cream in the butter with a spatula, then blend in 1 egg at a time, with a hand or stand mixer. Add all the other cake ingredients and mix well. Pour into the prepared pan.
3. Sprinkle with half the blueberries. Gently spread the cream cheese filling on the berries. Place the remaining blueberries on the cream cheese filling.
4. Combine all the topping ingredients. Stir with a fork or pastry blender until the mixture is crumbly. Sprinkle the streusel on the blueberries and bake for 45 to 50 minutes. When it is done, the cake should be pulling away from the edges of the pan and be slightly golden around the edges.
5. Do not remove the cake from the oven, as the temperature change may cause the cake to deflate. Instead, turn off the oven, open the door slightly, and allow the temperature to gradually reduce. The cake should be ready to be removed after 10 minutes. Allow the cake to completely cool before removing it from the pan.

NOTE: If using frozen berries, add them, still frozen, at the last minute. Frozen berries may affect the outcome of the cake as there will be extra liquid.
If the top of the cake browns too soon, tent the top with aluminum foil.
Substitute the blueberries with any berry.

DESSERT | 211

Boston Cream Poke Cake

FOR THE CAKE
2 cups almond flour
3/4 cup powdered sweetener
1 tbsp egg white powder
2 tsp cream of tartar
1 tsp baking soda
1/2 tsp xanthan gum
1/4 tsp nutmeg
2/3 cup butter
3 large eggs
1 tsp pure vanilla extract
1/2 cup whipping cream
5 drops liquid stevia, or to taste

FOR THE BOSTON CREAM
1/2 cup whipping cream
2 tbsp butter
1/2 cup powdered sweetener
4 large egg yolks, whisked
1 tsp pure vanilla extract
1/8 tsp xanthan gum (optional)

FOR THE GANACHE
2 oz unsweetened baking chocolate, chopped in small pieces
1/2 cup whipping cream
1/8-1/4 cup powdered sweetener (optional)
1 tbsp butter

A poke cake is a way to poke even more yummy goodness into what is already there. Here, the extra yummy comes in the form of   . A basic white cake is combined with sweet Boston cream and topped with a bitter ganache. All the flavours in a Boston cream donut have been tweaked just a little healthier and then twisted into a cake. Add sweetener to the ganache if desired but try to keep the amount of sweetness as low as possible and let the bitter chocolate nuances sing against the sweet cake and cream.

To prepare the cake
1. Preheat the oven to 350°F. Mix the dry ingredients, including the sweetener, in a mixing bowl. Cream in the butter, then mix in 1 egg at a time with a hand or stand mixer. Add all the remaining cake ingredients and mix well. Pour into a greased 9-inch-diameter spring form pan and bake for 45 to 50 minutes. The cake should start pulling away from the edges of the pan when it is done and should be golden around the edges.
2. Do not take the cake from the oven right away, as the change in temperature may cause it to deflate. Instead, turn off the oven, open the oven door slightly, and allow the temperature to gradually reduce. The cake should be ready to be removed after about 10 minutes. Do not remove the cake from the spring form pan until fully assembled and the ganache has set.

To prepare the Boston cream
1. Place the egg yolks in a bowl and whisk in the sweetener. Set aside.
2. Place the whipping cream and butter in a saucepan on a low-medium heat until the butter has melted and the cream starts to steam. Do not boil. Remove from the heat.
3. Temper the egg yolks by slowly drizzling 1 cup of the hot cream into the egg yolk bowl to avoid scrambling the eggs. Whisk the yolk mixture into the cream.
4. Return the cream mixture to a low heat. Sprinkle in the xanthan gum (if using) a little at a time. When the mixture begins to thicken, remove it from the heat and stir in the vanilla. The custard is ready when it coats the back of a spoon. Set aside to slightly cool while making the ganache.

To assemble
Poke holes down through the cake with the round handle of a wooden spoon. The holes should be at most 1 inch apart. Pour the Boston cream filling into the holes and on the top of the cake. Refrigerate for at least 1/2 hour before topping with the ganache. When ganache has set, remove cake from the pan and place on a cake stand or plate.

DESSERT

To prepare the ganache
1. Place the chocolate in a small bowl and set aside.
2. Heat the whipping cream in a medium saucepan on a medium heat, whisking so that the cream does not scorch. Remove from the heat as soon as the cream starts to steam. Do not boil.
3. Pour the hot cream over the chocolate and add the sweetener, if using.
4. Add the butter and whisk until fully combined.
5. Drizzle the warm ganache on the cake. Refrigerate immediately to set the chocolate.

NOTE: The ganache is meant to be a bitter chocolate topping that is well balanced against the sweet cake and Boston cream. Add the sweetener for a sweeter option. Some sweeteners recrystallize easily and do not work well in custards.

DESSERT | 215

Chocolate Chip Cookie Skillet

2 cups almond flour
1 cup powdered sweetener, or to taste
1 tsp cream of tartar
1/2 tsp salt
1/2 tsp baking soda
1/4 tsp xanthan gum
1/2 cup butter, at room temperature
2 large eggs
1 tsp pure vanilla extract
3/4 cup whipping cream
3/4 cup milk chocolate chips
1 oz unsweetened baking chocolate, chopped (optional)

What's not to love about a giant-sized chocolate chip cookie? The really nice thing about this recipe (besides the taste, of course) is that you don't have to worry about perfectly formed cookies, or if the batter will rise the right amount. You just mix it all up and dump it in an oven-safe skillet and let 'er go.

This oversized cookie is a great birthday cake alternative, a Sunday dessert, or just for someone who loves chocolate chip cookies.

Serve this warm with a dollop of cream cheese icing or ice cream (page 237) or serve cold.

1. Preheat the oven to 350°F.
2. Whisk together all the dry ingredients, including the sweetener. Stir in the remaining ingredients except the chocolate and mix well. Fold in the chocolate with a spatula. Transfer the batter to a 10- or 12-inch-diameter oven-safe skillet and bake for 20 to 25 minutes, then rotate the pan in the oven and bake for another 10 to 12 minutes. The cookie is done when the edges begin to turn brown and the inside is set when the pan is jiggled.

NOTE: If the edges start to brown, cover with aluminum foil. The smaller the pan, the thicker the batter, which means a longer cooking time. Adjust the cooking time accordingly. The unsweetened baking chocolate adds bitter tones which will affect the sweetness level of this cookie. If adding this optional ingredient, adjust the batter to taste.

Chocolate Faux Guinness Cake
WITH IRISH WHISKEY FROSTING

▶ **OPTIONAL: CHOCOLATE SAUCE**

FOR THE CAKE
2 cups almond flour
1 cup powdered sweetener
3/4 cup cocoa powder
3 tsp instant coffee powder
1 1/2 tsp cream of tartar
1 tsp baking soda
1/2 tsp xanthan gum
1 cup butter, at room temperature
1 cup whipping cream
2 tsp apple cider or white vinegar
2/3 cup sour cream
3 large eggs
1 tbsp pure vanilla extract

FOR THE IRISH CREAM
8 oz cream cheese, at room temperature
1 1/4 cups powdered sweetener
1/2 cup whipping cream
2 tbsp Irish whiskey (optional), or 1 tsp rum extract
1/8 tsp salt

The original Guinness cake is made with a bottle of Guinness or stout. We add a little coffee to enrich the chocolate vibe the same way that the dark ale would. Other substitutes to consider include a reduced mushroom stock/broth, coconut sauce, or bitter unsweetened chocolate. Either will add subtle notes of umami or savoury depth of flavour to this cake. Add a wee bit of Irish to the frosting to bring the finishing touch home to Ireland, where Guinness was born.

This recipe is fun to dress. Instead of perfectly coiffing the icing, haphazardly dollop the icing on the cake to resemble the froth on a poured Guinness Ale.

Make it to impress your guests at your next special occasion.

To make the cake
1. Preheat the oven to 350°F and line a 9-inch springform pan with parchment paper.
2. Combine all the dry ingredients, including the sweetener, in a large mixing bowl. Cream in the butter and then whisk in the remaining ingredients. Pour the cake batter into the prepared pan and bake for 45 minutes to 1 hour. Allow the cake to fully cool in the pan.

To prepare the Irish cream
Thoroughly mix all the ingredients together with a hand or stand mixer. Spread on the chilled cake so that it resembles the frothy top of a freshly poured pint.

▶ **OPTIONAL: CHOCOLATE SAUCE**
1 tsp instant coffee powder
3/4 cup brewed coffee
3 tbsp dark cocoa powder
4 oz cream cheese
10-12 drops liquid stevia
4 oz unsweetened baking chocolate, chopped and melted
1/4 cup powdered sweetener
2 tsp oil
2 tbsp hot water

1. Place the brewed coffee in a small saucepan and add the instant coffee. On a medium heat, reduce the coffee to half its volume. Remove from the heat and stir in the cocoa powder and sweeteners until smooth. Slowly whisk the coffee mixture into the melted chocolate until smooth.
2. If the sauce starts to separate, drizzle in the water while whisking. It may take 2 to 3 tablespoons to bring the sauce back.

Cinnamon Coffee Cake Loaf

FOR THE CAKE

2 1/4 cups almond flour
1 cup powdered sweetener
1 tsp cream of tartar
1/2 tsp baking soda
1/2 tsp xanthan gum
1/4 tsp salt
1/2 cup butter, at room temperature (not melted)
3 large eggs, at room temperature
1/4 cup plus 2 tbsp whipping cream
2 tsp pure vanilla extract

FOR THE CINNAMON FILLING

1/2 cup granulated sweetener
1 1/2 tbsp Ceylon cinnamon
1/2 tsp allspice
1/8 tsp ground cardamom
1/8 tsp nutmeg
1/8 tsp salt

This soft and decadent loaf has a crispy crunchy cinnamon topping. The secret is the combination of powdered and granular sweeteners. Use powdered sweetener in the cake itself and a combination of both for the cinnamon filling. The delicate grit of the granular sweetener adds the right amount of crunch to that top coating. If you do not like a crunchy topping, substitute the granulated sweetener with an equal measure of powdered sweetener.

Be prepared to pop this one in the freezer right away so you don't overindulge!

1. Preheat the oven to 325°F. Line a 9-inch loaf pan with parchment paper.
2. Whisk the cinnamon filling ingredients together and set aside.
3. In a medium mixing bowl, whisk together the dry cake ingredients, including the sweetener. Cream the butter into the dry ingredients, then stir in the remaining wet ingredients. Mix well.
4. Spoon a little over half of the batter into the prepared loaf pan. Either smooth the batter flat or create a centre well in the batter.
5. Sprinkle about two-thirds of the cinnamon mixture on the bottom layer.
6. Add the extra whipping cream to the remaining batter to make it easier to spread on the cinnamon layer. Carefully spoon the remaining batter on the cinnamon mixture.
7. Sprinkle the remaining cinnamon mixture on the loaf.
8. Bake for 15 minutes, then reduce the heat to 300°F and bake for 30 to 40 minutes.
9. Let the loaf cool for 15 minutes before removing it from the pan.

NOTE: Granulated sweeteners can be powdered in a mini blender or coffee grinder to create a powdered sweetener. This loaf is best served cold.

Cranberry Cheesecake WITH WHITE CHOCOLATE MOUSSE

FOR THE CRANBERRY COMPOTE

2 cups fresh cranberries

1/2 cup powdered sweetener

1/4 tsp salt

water to cover the bottom of the pot

1 tbsp apple cider or white vinegar

1 tsp pure vanilla extract

FOR THE CRUST

2 cups almond flour

1/4 cup melted butter

2 tbsp powdered sweetener

1/8 tsp salt

FOR THE CHEESECAKE

1 32-oz container ricotta cheese

16 oz cream cheese, at room temperature

1 cup powdered sweetener

4 large eggs

1/8 cup lemon juice

2 tsp lemon zest (from 1 lemon), or 1 tsp dried lemon zest

1 tsp pure vanilla extract

1 tsp xanthan gum

1/4 tsp salt

FOR THE WHITE CHOCOLATE MOUSSE

8 oz white chocolate (page 295)

8 oz cream cheese, at room temperature

4 oz butter

1/2 cup powdered sweetener

1/2 tsp white chocolate extract

2 oz white chocolate, shaved, for garnish

This cheesecake gives perfectly balanced bites of creamy, tart, and sweet and just a hint of crunch (from the crust) with every bite.

Making cranberry compote may seem like extra work, but it allows the cook to control the level of sweetness and eliminate unwanted ingredients found in processed food. Find fresh cranberries in the produce section in the autumn and the freezer section during the off-season.

You can make this without the white chocolate mousse, but if you want the full effect the white chocolate mousse is a must.

To prepare the cranberry compote

1. Place the cranberries, sweetener, and salt in a saucepan on a medium heat. Add enough water to cover the bottom of the saucepan. Mix well and bring the water to a boil, then reduce the heat to low; simmer, stirring often, for 12 to 15 minutes. The berries will pop as they cook.
2. Add the vinegar and vanilla only after all the berries have popped and it has reached a thick, jamlike consistency.
3. Simmer for 10 more minutes, take the saucepan off the heat, and let the compote cool completely.

To prepare the crust

1. Preheat the oven to 325°F and line a 9-inch springform pan with parchment paper.
2. Combine all the crust ingredients and press into the prepared pan. Place the springform pan on a lipped baking sheet, as butter may seep out of the bottom of the pan while it is baking. Bake for 10 minutes, then rotate the pan. Bake for another 10 minutes or so, until very lightly browned. Remove from the oven and set aside to cool.

To prepare the cheesecake

1. Process all the cheesecake ingredients in a food processor until smooth.
2. Pour the mixture on the cooked base and tap gently to remove any air bubbles. Use a wooden spoon to smooth any air bubbles on the top of the cheesecake. Bake for 60 minutes or until lightly golden and just set. Do not open the door. Turn off the oven and leave the cheesecake there to cool for 60 minutes, with the oven door closed. Remove it from the oven and allow it to cool slightly. Cover with plastic wrap and refrigerate the cheesecake for at least 4 hours before adding the cooled cranberry compote.

To prepare the white chocolate mousse

1. Break the white chocolate into small pieces and melt in a double boiler.
2. Beat the cream cheese with a mixer for a few minutes. Drizzle in the melted white chocolate while continuing to beat the cream cheese. Mix well.
3. Spread or pipe the white chocolate mousse on the cranberry cheesecake. For a white-on-white top, separate the mousse into two batches and use one batch as a spread and one to decorate with a frosting tip.

Crustless Salted Caramel Cheesecake

FOR THE CARAMEL SAUCE

1 cup allulose or a monk fruit and erythritol blend sweetener

1 cup butter, at room temperature

1 cup whipping cream

FOR THE CHEESECAKE

24 oz cream cheese, at room temperature

1 cup sour cream, at room temperature

4 large eggs, at room temperature

3/4 cup powdered sweetener

3/4 cup caramel sauce (above), cooled to room temperature

1 tsp pure vanilla extract

This special occasion cheesecake can be made with a crust (see Notes below), or keep it crustless to reduce the carb count.

If there was ever a recipe that needs room-temperature ingredients, it's this one. Plan ahead and take all the ingredients out of the refrigerator early; otherwise, your cheesecake will not produce perfect results. Make the caramel sauce ahead of time, as one-third of the cooled sauce is added to the cheesecake base.

If you're expecting company, hold off on adding the sauce. Plate the individual piece of cake and pour on the sauce tableside and finish each with finishing salt, sprinkled high and wide with a flourish.

To prepare the caramel sauce

1. Heat the butter in a saucepan on a medium heat until it comes to a rolling boil. Continue to boil until it darkens, with tiny specks of brown visible. This browned butter will create flavour; do not be afraid to let it darken.
2. Quickly add the sweetener and the cream to the browned butter. Whisk until the sauce is smooth. Reduce the heat and simmer for 5 minutes without stirring. Remove from the heat, whisk thoroughly, and set aside to cool. The caramel will thicken as it cools.

To prepare the cheesecake

1. Preheat the oven to 325°F.
2. Place a sheet of parchment paper on a 9-inch springform pan base before attaching it to the top section. When attached, trim the parchment edges so that 1/2 inch hangs out of the pan. Line the sides of the pan with parchment paper for easy cleanup.
3. Combine all the ingredients in a medium mixing bowl and mix on high for 5 to 7 minutes or until the batter is very smooth. Pour into the prepared pan and bake for 1 1/4 to 1 1/2 hours. The cake is done when it is golden brown on top, the centre has a slight jiggle, and the edges pull away from the sides of the pan.
4. Turn the oven off, leaving the cheesecake inside with the door ajar for 20 to 30 minutes. Remove the cheesecake from the oven and completely cool.

To assemble

Pour the caramel sauce on the cooled cheesecake. Refrigerate the cheesecake for at least 3 to 4 hours to set. Sprinkle with a pinch of sea salt before serving. Serve cold.

NOTE: Allulose or a monk fruit blend sweetener are the best choices, as some sweeteners recrystallize easily and could ruin a cheesecake or caramel. Want a crust for this cheesecake? Combine 1 1/2 cups almond flour, 2 tablespoons powdered sweetener, a pinch of salt, and 1/4 cup melted butter. Press into the bottom of the prepared pan and bake at 300°F for 10 minutes, then rotate the pan and bake for another 10 minutes. Cool before loading the cheesecake.

Dark Chocolate Tart WITH RASPBERRY COULIS
❖ **VARIATION: NO-BAKE GANACHE FILLING**

FOR THE CRUST
1 recipe pie crust (page 56)
3 tbsp cocoa powder

FOR THE MOUSSE
12 oz unsweetened baking or dark chocolate (70% cocoa solids), finely chopped
1/2 cup butter, chopped
3 large eggs
large egg yolks
1 1/2 cups powdered sweetener
1 tsp cream of tartar

FOR THE RASPBERRY COULIS
1 cup fresh or frozen raspberries
1/2 cup powdered sweetener
2 tbsp lemon juice
1/4 tsp salt

18-20 raspberries, for garnish
edible flowers, for garnish

I am without question a bona fide chocoholic. In my younger years, I had eyes only for milk chocolate, but as my palate grew, I began to get a real appreciation for the real stuff: dark chocolate.

The term *terroir*, once used exclusively with wines, has recently been adopted by chocolatiers. It attributes the subtle nuances of flavour to a "sense of place," heavily influenced by the climate, soil makeup, and harvesting and roasting techniques. Chocolate can be fruity, nutty, floral, or earthy, and terroir leaves its mark on the flavour of each chocolate.

I faced a dilemma with this recipe: do I go with a baked or a no-bake chocolate tart? I say, why choose any version? Try them both.

To prepare the crust
Preheat the oven to 350°F and grease a 9-inch round fluted tart pan with Baker's Magic (Pan) Release (page 273). Place a lipped baking sheet beneath the tart pan to catch any melted butter. Follow the blind-baking instructions on page 56.

To prepare the mousse
1. Place the chocolate and butter in a metal bowl over a saucepan of water on a medium heat and stir occasionally until it is melted and totally smooth. Do not let the bottom of the pan touch the water.
2. Set aside the chocolate to cool slightly but keep the pan of water on the heat.
3. In another metal bowl, place the eggs, egg yolks, sweetener, and salt and use a hand mixer to whip for about 10 to 15 minutes or until nearly tripled in volume and the mixture reaches the ribbon stage, where the whisk is lifted over the mixture and the batter falls slowly into a ribbon that holds its shape for a few minutes.
4. Remove from the heat. Gently fold one-third of the chocolate mixture into the whisked eggs until just incorporated. Add the next one-third and fold in. Repeat the process one more time with the remaining batter.
5. Immediately pour the mousse into the prebaked shell and smooth with an offset spatula. Bake for 18 to 20 minutes or until just set.

To prepare the raspberry coulis
Combine the raspberries, sweetener, water, and lemon juice in a saucepan on a low-medium heat. Cook and stir until the raspberries are soft and have released their juices. Remove from the heat and allow to cool slightly. Transfer to a fine sieve over a bowl and allow the raspberry liquid syrup to flow through. Return to the saucepan to reduce to the desired consistency.

NOTE: Mix the eggs and yolks with a hand mixer on a medium speed for about 5 to 6 minutes. A high-quality 70 per cent cacao chocolate is recommended.

❖ **VARIATION: NO-BAKE GANACHE FILLING**

12 oz dark chocolate (70% cocoa content)
1 cup whipping cream
4 tbsp butter, at room temperature
1 1/2 cups powdered sweetener

1. Place the chopped chocolate in a large bowl. Set aside.
2. In a small saucepan on a low-medium heat, bring the cream to the point of steaming. Do not let it boil. Pour the hot cream over the chopped chocolate and leave for 2 to 3 minutes without stirring. Add the butter and sweetener and stir with a wooden spoon or spatula until combined and smooth. Pour into the cooled tart shell and refrigerate for 1 to 2 hours.
3. Sprinkle with sea salt.

Double Chocolate Peanut Butter Bars

FOR THE BASE

1 1/2 cups almond flour
1/4 cup butter, at room temperature
2 tbsp powdered sweetener
2 tbsp cocoa powder
1/4 tsp salt

FOR THE PEANUT BUTTER FILLING

2 cups almond flour
1 cup butter, at room temperature
1 cup natural peanut butter
3/4 cup powdered sweetener

FOR THE CHOCOLATE TOPPING

8 oz unsweetened baking chocolate
1/3 cup powdered sweetener
3 tbsp natural peanut butter
1/4 cup butter
1 tbsp oil

If you are a peanut-butter-cup or peanut-butter-ball fan, this one has your name written all over it. This recipe has all the taste you love, with a no-fuss approach to forming perfectly shaped balls and ensuring that the chocolate coating is just so on your cookie. In fact, our preference is to serve them rustic and real—we both love the little jagged imperfect pieces best of all!

This dessert is not too sweet (you can increase the sweetener for your own family's taste) and has creamy peanut butter and loads of chocolate crunch.

1. Preheat the oven to 300°F and line a 9- by 13-inch pan with parchment paper.
2. Combine all the base ingredients and press into the prepared pan. Place a piece of aluminum foil over the top so that the crust does not burn. Bake for 10 to 15 minutes. Remove the foil, turn off the oven, and return the crust to the oven for 5 minutes under residual heat. Remove from the heat and set aside to cool.
3. In a medium bowl, combine the peanute butter filling ingredients and mix well. Spread evenly on the cooled base. Set aside.
4. For the topping, place the chocolate and peanut butter in a microwave-safe bowl and microwave in 15-second bursts until it is fully melted. Spread the chocolate topping on the peanut butter mixture evenly. Refrigerate for at least 60 minutes. Cut in pieces and serve.

NOTE: Try making this in a 9- by 9-inch baking pan and cut in 1-inch bites. For a no-bake version, skip the crunchy base, line the bottom of a pan with parchment, and start with the peanut butter layer. As peanuts are legumes and are classified as an inflammatory food, consume them or peanut butter in moderation. Substitute the peanut butter with almond butter to avoid this concern, and enjoy a more neutral-tasting treat.

Faux Apple Cake
❖ **VARIATION: APPLE COFFEE CAKE**

FOR THE CARAMEL APPLE

3/4 cup butter
1/2 cup packed brown sweetener
1/2 cup powdered sweetener
1 tsp Ceylon cinnamon
1/2 tsp allspice
1/2 tsp ground cardamom (optional)
1/4 tsp ground ginger
1 tsp pure vanilla extract
2 medium chayote squash, peeled, sliced, and parboiled

FOR THE CAKE

2 1/2 cups almond flour
1 cup powdered sweetener
2 tbsp egg white powder
1 tsp cream of tartar
1/2 tsp baking soda
1/2 tsp xanthan gum
1 1/2 tsp Ceylon cinnamon
1/2 tsp nutmeg
1/2 cup butter
2 large eggs
2 tsp pure vanilla extract
3/4 cup whipping cream

FOR THE CINNAMON MIX

1/8 cup powdered sweetener
1/8 cup granulated sweetener
2 tsp Ceylon cinnamon
1 tsp allspice

The upside-down version of this cake will wow guests with a gorgeous top of layered faux apples (chayote squash) and caramel. It's ooey gooey and decadent and your company will love it. The other version—an Apple Coffee Cake, with layers of apples through the middle—is just pure family comfort food.

Chayote squash is similar to apples in texture but without the sweetness; in fact, they look like a cross between a Granny Smith apple and an odd-shaped pear. The big difference is that chayote squash has a much lower carb count than apples—and lets you control how much (and which) sweetener you use.

To prepare the caramel apple
1. Line a 2-inch-deep, 9-inch-diameter pan (do not use a springform pan, as the caramel sauce will drain out) with parchment paper.
2. Place the butter in a small saucepan on a medium heat. Whisk occasionally until the butter has melted and begins to brown. Brown flecks should appear in the bottom of the pan.
3. When the butter has browned, add the sweetener and the spices and continue to cook, whisking constantly for 1 minute as the mixture thickens. Remove from the heat and whisk in the vanilla extract.
4. Pour the caramel into the prepared pan. Arrange the chayote slices neatly on the caramel, overlapping where necessary. Sprinkle the cinnamon mix on the chayote slices.
5. Refrigerate the pan for a few minutes while preparing the cake batter. This sets the topping arrangement.

To prepare the cake
1. Preheat the oven to 350°F.
2. Combine all the dry ingredients, including the sweetener, in a large mixing bowl. Cream the butter into the dry mixture, then whisk in the remaining ingredients. Set aside.
3. Pour the cake batter on the cooled caramel and apple mixture and carefully spread it out.
4. Bake for 20 minutes and then reduce the temperature to 300°F. Bake for 30 to 35 minutes or until a toothpick inserted in the cake comes out clean.
5. Allow the cake to cool to room temperature, then refrigerate to allow it to cool completely before flipping it. Top the pan with a plate or serving platter and flip.

NOTE: Substitute chayote with peeled zucchini. Adjust the sweetness level to taste. This cake is best served cold. Use allulose for a caramel that does not recrystallize. When reheating the caramel, whisk a splash of whipping cream vigorously into the sauce just before serving.

✔ **TIP**

If the cake sticks to the pan, place hot water in the sink, just enough to go halfway up the sides of the pan. Place the pan carefully in the water for 5 minutes for the caramel to soften (the cinnamon becomes fragrant as it heats). Wipe off the water and quickly flip the cake onto the plate while the caramel is still warm.

❖ **VARIATION: APPLE COFFEE CAKE**

In a Bundt cake pan coated with Baker's Magic (Pan) Release (page 273), place half the batter in the bottom and cover with half the cinnamon mix. Then add a caramel apple layer, followed by the other half of the cinnamon mix, then the remaining batter. Follow the baking instructions above.

DESSERT | 235

French Vanilla Ice Cream
❖ **MULTIPLE VARIATIONS**

6 large egg yolks
1/2 cup powdered allulose or alternate powdered sweetener, divided
10-12 drops liquid stevia
1/4 tsp salt
3 cups whipping cream
1 vanilla bean
1 tsp pure vanilla extract

Many of us love ice cream, but starting on a journey of health means asking what else (modifying agents, emulsifiers, and stabilizers, added sugar …) manufacturers put in the commercially available versions of this frozen dessert.

If you're going beyond the vanilla base and adding fruit, make sure you partially cook the additions to reduce any extra water that is found naturally in the fruit. This water will freeze as ice crystals and won't play well with your ice cream.

The process of taking cream and sweetener and transforming it into a custard and then churning that into your own frozen dessert sensation is worth the extra effort involved.

1. In a large glass bowl, whisk the yolks, half of the sweetener, and the salt.
2. Combine the cream and the remaining sweetener in a medium saucepan. Cut the vanilla bean in half lengthwise and scrape out the seeds. Add both to the cream. Heat the cream on a low-medium heat, stirring occasionally until it starts to steam. Remove from the heat and remove 1 cup of the hot cream. Slowly whisk the hot cream into the egg to avoid scrambling the eggs.
3. When the egg is tempered, slowly pour the mixture back into the hot cream. Cook on a low-medium heat, stirring constantly, until the custard reaches 170° to 175°F and lightly coats the back of a spoon.
4. Remove from the heat and set aside to cool, stirring occasionally as it cools.
5. Refrigerate for at least 4 hours or overnight. Remove the vanilla bean. Churn in an ice cream machine according to the manufacturer's instructions.
6. Transfer to the freezer for at least 4 hours, or ideally overnight.

✔ **TIP**
Custard at the spoon-coating stage is a crème anglaise or pouring custard, which can be used for crème brûlée or cream pie filling.

NOTE: Instead of an ice cream maker, use a large freezer bag or a Mason jar to shake and agitate the crème anglaise every 15 minutes until it is set. It can also be whipped with a hand or stand mixer to aerate it before freezing. Add any berries or mix-ins (from the variations) during the last 5 minutes of churning.

❖ VARIATIONS

Cherry Chocolate Ice Cream

2 tsp pure almond extract (to replace the vanilla extract)
15-20 cherries, pitted and diced, or berries of choice
1 oz unsweetened baking chocolate, shaved

1. Place the cherries in a small sauté pan with just enough water to cover the bottom, and simmer to remove as much water as possible from them.
2. Add the cherries and chocolate to the ice cream in the last 5 minutes of churning.
3. Freeze for at least 4 hours or ideally overnight.

Maple Pecan Ice Cream

3 tsp maple extract (to replace the vanilla extract)
1/4 cup maple syrup substitute (page 283) (optional)
1/8 cup chopped, roasted pecans, roasted

1. Add the maple syrup substitute to the base after it has been cooked and before it is refrigerated.
2. Add the pecans in the last 5 minutes of churning.

Orange Chocolate Ice Cream

zest of 1 orange
3-4 drops orange oil, or 1 tsp orange extract
1 tbsp orange blossom water
1 oz unsweetened baking chocolate, shaved

Add all the ingredients (except the chocolate) to the base and then heat. Add the chocolate in the last 5 minutes of churning.

Butter Pecan Ice Cream

maple extract (to replace the vanilla extract)
2/3 cup chopped pecans
1/4 cup butter
1/4 cup allulose
1/4 cup brown allulose

1. Sauté the pecans in butter until the butter is browned. Strain the pecans and freeze. Pour off the butter, leaving the really dark bits in the pan. Let the browned butter cool and solidify.
2. Add the cooled butter after tempering the eggs and add the pecans in the last 5 minutes of churning.

Addie's Cream (coffee-flavoured)

2 tsp espresso powder or instant coffee powder

Add the coffee to the yolks and then temper.

Chocolate Fudge

4 tbsp cocoa powder (3 regular and 1 dark)
1 tsp chocolate extract (+ 1 tsp pure vanilla extract)

Add the cocoa to the yolks and then temper.

Ginger Crème Brûlée

6 large egg yolks
1/2 cup powdered sweetener, halved
1/4 tsp salt
3 cups whipping cream
2 tbsp fresh ginger, or 1 tsp ground ginger
1 tsp pure vanilla extract

This creamy baked custard has a delicate hint of ginger and a brûléed top.

When we decided to seek a healthier lifestyle, I thought crème brûlée was an indulgence that was lost to us. I mean, how could you possibly get that candied top without the sugar? So, we went without.

But when I developed this ginger custard recipe, I knew I had to give that candied top a go. I tried all kinds of fancy sweetener variations and combinations. None of them produced the results that I needed. As a last resort, I went back to basics, to that monk fruit and erythritol blend that we are used to.

1. In a large bowl, whisk the yolks, half of the sweetener, and salt. Set aside.
2. Combine the cream and remaining sweetener in a medium saucepan. Heat on a low-medium heat, stirring occasionally, until it starts to steam. Take off the heat and remove 1 cup of the hot cream. Slowly whisk this hot cream into the egg. When the egg has been tempered, slowly whisk the mixture back into the saucepan. Add the vanilla and ginger. Cook on a low-medium heat, stirring constantly until the custard reaches 170° to 175°F and lightly coats the back of a spoon. Do not let the mixture boil.
3. Turn off the heat and allow the ginger to steep for at least 20 minutes, or longer to infuse more flavour. Remove the ginger (if using fresh) from the custard.
4. Position a rack in the centre of the oven and preheat the oven to 350°F.
5. Bring a kettle of water to a boil. Put 12 4-ounce ramekins in a roasting pan or baking dish that is at least as deep as the ramekins. Divide the custard among the ramekins.
6. Slowly pour hot water from a kettle into the pan (do not splash water in the ramekins) until it comes about two-thirds of the way up the sides of the ramekins.
7. Carefully transfer the pan to the oven and bake until the custards are set around the edges but still slightly jiggly in the centre, about 35 to 40 minutes.
8. Transfer the ramekins to a cooling rack and let cool at room temperature for 30 minutes. Refrigerate the baked custards uncovered.
9. Once the custards are refrigerator-cold, wrap each ramekin with plastic wrap. Refrigerate for at least 3 hours or up to 2 days before proceeding with the brûléed top.
10. To brûlée, sprinkle 1 to 1 1/2 teaspoons of the remaining sweetener evenly on each custard. Wipe any residual sweetener off the ramekin rims.
11. Light a culinary or mini blowtorch and hold the flame 2 to 3 inches from the top of the custard, slowly gliding it back and forth over the surface until the sweetener melts and turns a deep golden brown. Allow to cool and harden for 1 minute or so, then serve immediately.

NOTE: Do not use allulose for the brûlée, as the top will not crisp up. A monk fruit and erythritol combination is the preferred sweetener.

Jamaican Rum Cake

FOR THE CAKE

2 1/4 cups almond flour

1 1/4 cups powdered sweetener

1 1/2 tsp cream of tartar

3/4 tsp baking soda

1 tsp xanthan gum

1/2 tsp salt

1/2 cup butter, at room temperature

1/4 cup olive oil

1/2 cup whipping cream

1/8 cup apple cider or white vinegar

4 large eggs

1 tbsp pure vanilla extract

1/3 cup white rum

FOR THE RUM AND BUTTER SYRUP

1/4 cup butter

1/2 cup powdered sweetener

1/4 cup water

1/2 cup white rum

1 tsp pure vanilla extract

The best cake I have ever tasted was a Jamaican rum cake: it was super moist with a hint of rum and full of flavour. It reminded me of the Christmas fruit cakes that I grew up with, without the fruit and spices.

This basic rum cake can be made chocolate, gingerbread, red velvet, or lemon.

To prepare the cake
1. Preheat the oven to 350°F and line a Bundt pan or cake pan with parchment paper or use Baker's Magic (Pan) Release (page 273).
2. Combine all the dry ingredients, including the sweetener, in a large mixing bowl. Cream in the butter and then whisk in the oil and add the remaining cake ingredients. Pour the batter into the prepared pan and bake for 50 to 65 minutes or until a wooden toothpick inserted in the centre comes out clean.
3. Completely cool the cake.

To prepare the rum and butter syrup
1. Place all the syrup ingredients in a saucepan on a low-medium heat. Simmer for 7 or 8 minutes and remove from the heat. Set aside to cool.
2. Poke holes in the cake with a skewer. Pour the rum sauce on the cake.
3. Cover with plastic wrap and refrigerate for at least 6 hours.

NOTE: Replace the rum with 3 tablespoons rum extract if a non-alcoholic version is preferred.

DESSERT | 243

Lilac Love Cake

❖ **VARIATION: S'PIKED LILAC LEMONADE**

FOR THE LILAC SYRUP
2 heaping cups fresh lilac petals
1 cup water
1/2 cup powdered sweetener, or to taste

FOR THE LILAC CAKE
2 cups almond flour
1 cup powdered sweetener
1/4 cup egg white powder
1 tsp cream of tartar
1/2 tsp baking soda
1/2 tsp xanthan gum
1/2 tsp sea salt
1/2 cup butter, at room temperature
1 cup fresh lilac petals
3 large eggs
3/4 cup whipping cream
2 tsp pure vanilla extract

FOR THE FROSTING
12 oz cream cheese, at room temperature
½ cup butter, at room temperature
3/4 cup powdered sweetener
1 tsp pure vanilla extract or rosewater
1/4 tsp salt

FOR THE STICKY LILACS
1/4 cup fresh lilac petals
1 large egg white
1/2 cup granulated sweetener

I just love this cake—the look, the feel, the taste, the very idea of it is almost romantic.

Know what else gives me the warm and fuzzies? Learning to forage in our backyard and take advantage of what mother nature offers us. Learning to grow our own food (and foraging natural foods) is such a rewarding venture. And any steps we take toward food stability and growing our own sustenance will enrich our health and our lives.

Forage in a clean area and always be certain that what you are about to eat is edible. Even when flowers are listed as edible, sometimes the stems and roots are not. For example, a dandelion plant is 100 per cent edible—the roots, the stem, and the flowers are edible; but only the flowers of wisteria are edible, while the rest of the plant is toxic.

To prepare the lilac syrup
1. Place the sweetener and water in a medium saucepan on a medium-high heat and bring to a boil. Reduce the heat, add the petals, cover, and simmer for 20 to 30 minutes. Turn off the heat and let the saucepan sit on the stovetop for at least 2 hours.
2. Refrigerate the syrups with the petals overnight for a more robust lilac flavour.

To prepare the lilac cake
1. Preheat the oven to 350°F. Line the bottom of the cake pan and coat with a layer of Baker's Magic (Pan) Release (page 273).
2. Combine all the dry ingredients and then cream the butter into the mixture. Add the wet ingredients and whisk thoroughly. Use a spatula to gently fold in the lilac petals. Pour the batter into the prepared pan and bake for 35 to 40 minutes, or until a toothpick inserted in the centre comes out clean. Let the cake cool for at least 20 minutes before turning it out.

To prepare the frosting
Mix all the ingredients with a hand or stand mixer until smooth.

To prepare the sticky lilacs
Using plating tongs or tweezers, dip each lilac petal in the egg white and then in the sweetener. Place each petal on parchment paper to dry for several hours.

To assemble
Frost the cooled cake and place the sticky lilacs on the top or the sides of the cake with tongs.

DESSERT | 245

❖ VARIATION: S'PIKED LILAC LEMONADE

1/4 cup lilac syrup (see page 244)
1/8 cup lemon juice
3 tbsp vodka (optional)
3 or 4 drops lemon essential oil
1 tsp powdered sweetener, or to taste
carbonated water or club soda

Place the first five ingredients in a cocktail shaker or Mason jar loaded with ice, then shake, strain, and pour into a fancy glass. Top with carbonated water and lilac petals.

NOTE: Lemon water enhancer can be used instead of lemon essence/extract. Add 3 to 4 drops lemon essential oil to the cake for a lemony twist.

Edible Flowers

1. Never gather flowers from roadsides or train tracks, as these areas are often sprayed with growth-retardant chemicals.
2. Do not eat store-bought flowers unless they are from a certified organic grower or specialty gourmet shop. Those sold at florists and greenhouses have likely been treated with fertilizers and pesticides.
3. Just because a flower is edible does not mean that the plant is good to eat.
4. If you have never eaten raw flowers and do not know if you are allergic to them, take a nibble before you eat a whole bouquet. Always wash well.

Here's our list of favourite floral edibles. For a more comprehensive list of edible flowers visit the website of gardening experts Thompson Morgan.

Apple / crabapple blossoms	Begonia
Dianthus / carnation / pinks	Campanula
Citrus tree blossoms	Dahlia
Daisy	Evening primrose
Forget-me-not	Gladiolus
Herb blossoms	Honeysuckle
Lavender	Lemon balm
Lilac	Marigold
Nasturtium	Pansy
Peony	Rose
Poppy	Strawberry blossoms
Viola and violet	

DESSERT | 247

Lime Chiffon Cake *WITH PRALINE CRUMB*

➤ **EXTRA: MINTY RUM SYRUP**

FOR THE PECAN PRALINE CRUMB
1/2 cup powdered sweetener
1/4 cup butter
1 cup roughly chopped pecans
1/8 tsp salt

FOR THE CAKE
2 cups almond flour
1/4 cup coconut flour
1 tbsp egg white powder
1 tsp baking soda
1/4 tsp xanthan gum
1/2 cup butter, at room temperature
6 large egg yolks
zest of 1 1/2 limes
6 large egg whites
2 tsp cream of tartar
1 cup powdered sweetener
juice of 1 1/2 limes

FOR THE BUTTERCREAM ICING
1 cup butter, at room temperature
1 1/2 cups powdered sweetener
4 oz cream cheese, at room temperature
1 tsp pure vanilla extract
zest and juice of 1 1/2 limes
pinch of salt

FOR THE GARNISH
1 lime, thinly sliced

Chiffon, a type of foam cake, is partially leavened by whipping egg whites to create volume. The resulting texture is a light, airy, spongy cake that is extremely soft and fluffy. In a gluten-free and health-savvy kitchen, the extra leaveners—the cream of tartar and baking soda—also help to lift the heavier flours.

Our cakes won't have the same lift as those baked using traditional ingredients. What's important is the flavour profile—and this lime-flavoured recipe is spectacular. It can be made without the praline crumb for an easier family dessert, but the praline makes the recipe sing like it's centre stage at the opera.

Make sure to include the optional mojito syrup (in the recipe extra) if you have company coming and you want a fancy dessert.

To prepare the pecan praline crumb
1. Line a baking tray with parchment paper.
2. Melt the sweetener, salt, and butter in a medium sauté pan on a medium-high heat. Swirl the pan to move the sweetener but do not stir. When the sweetener is liquid, bring it to a boil and continue to cook until a caramel colour is reached. Keep the pan moving, being careful not to burn the caramel. Add the pecans and swirl the pan to coat them in the caramel, and then pour the entire mixture into the prepared baking tray. Refrigerate to cool. When the mixture has completely cooled, smash with a rolling pin into pieces and then pulse the pieces in a blender or food processor until the mix resembles a crumb. Set aside.

To prepare the cake
1. Preheat the oven to 350°F and line a Bundt or round cake pan with Baker's Magic (Pan) Release (page 273). Set aside.
2. Whisk all the dry ingredients together, then cream in the butter, followed by the remaining batter ingredients. Set the batter aside.
3. Place the egg whites and cream of tartar in a large mixing bowl. With a hand mixer, start beating on a very low speed and increase the speed only when the egg whites are no longer expanding. Beating slowly will create small stable bubbles; if this process is rushed, the cake will fall. Slowly add the sweetener and lime juice when the whipping is nearly done.
4. You should be able to lift the whisk out of the bowl and set it upside down without the eggs falling off the whisk. The egg whites should form a peak with a slightly drooping tip.
5. Set two-thirds of the whisked egg whites aside.
6. Combine the batter with one-third of the egg whites. Pour the batter mixture around the sides of the bowl, about 1 inch from the edges of the bowl (not in the middle). With a spatula, gently fold the batter into the egg mixture, making figure 8 movements up through the centre of the batter. Avoid knocking the air out of the batter.

7. Next, very carefully incorporate another one-third of the remaining whisked eggs into the batter, then fold in the last of the whipped eggs. Gently pour the batter into the prepared pan. Do not knock the pan to remove the air bubbles. Bake for 25 to 35 minutes, rotating the pan halfway through the cooking time. The cake is cooked when a knife or skewer comes out of the centre clean. Turn off the oven and allow the pan to sit in place for 10 to 15 minutes, with the door ajar.
8. Remove the pan from the oven and invert it on a rack. Leave the cake in the upside-down pan on the rack for at least 15 minutes, then refrigerate it upside down for at least 30 minutes to cool before removing it from the pan. This will help prevent the cake from caving in.
9. While the cake is cooling, make the buttercream.

To prepare the buttercream icing
Place all the buttercream ingredients in a medium mixing bowl and mix with a hand or stand mixer until the icing is fluffy and thoroughly combined.

To assemble
Place the cooled cake on a cake plate. Ice the top with the buttercream. Refrigerate for 10 to 15 minutes to firm up. Sprinkle the pecan praline crumb on the cake top. Garnish with twisted lime slices.

✔ **TIP**
1. Ensure that there is no trace of yolk or oil in the whites. Use a glass bowl (never a plastic bowl) for whipping eggs.
2. Use room-temperature eggs to ensure that the egg whites whisk to peaks.
3. Eliminate any drafts circulating through the kitchen, which can make the cake collapse.
4. If using a round cake pan and not a Bundt pan, cut the cake into two layers when it is cooled. Use a piece of sewing thread drawn tight and pulled through the cooled cake or a cake knife to cut the cake. Spread the icing between the layers and then coat the outsides of the cooled cake with the pecan crumb. Pat the fallen crumbs onto the sides of the cake.

➤ **MINTY RUM SYRUP**
For a mojito twist, make a minty rum syrup to elevate this cake off the charts!
1/4 cup brown sweetener
1/4 cup water
3 tbsp white rum, or 2 tsp rum extract
zest and juice of 1/2 lime
8-10 mint leaves

1. Place all the ingredients except the zest and mint in a medium saucepan on a low heat. Cook until the sweetener dissolves, then turn up the heat and boil for 3 to 5 minutes until the syrup thickens. Remove from the heat and add the zest and mint leaves.
2. Set aside for the flavours to marry. When cool (and ready to finish the cake), remove the solids.
3. Brush the cake with the strained syrup before placing the icing on the layers. Be generous to ensure that the cake is moist.

Lisa and Brett's Nanaimo Cheesecake

FOR THE PASTRY CREAM
5 large egg yolks
1/2 cup powdered sweetener
pinch of salt
1 1/3 cups whipping cream
2 tbsp butter
2 tsp pure vanilla extract

FOR THE CRUST
1 1/2 cups almond flour
1/4 cup cocoa powder
1/4 cup powdered sweetener
1/2 tsp salt
1/8 tsp nutmeg
1/2 cup butter, at room temperature
1 large egg, whisked
3/4 cup unsweetened fine shredded coconut
1/2 cup chopped pecans or walnuts
1 tsp pure vanilla extract

FOR THE VANILLA FILLING
12 oz cream cheese, at room temperature
1/2 cup butter, at room temperature
cooled pastry cream (recipe above)
3/4 cup powdered sweetener
1 tsp pure vanilla extract

FOR THE CHOCOLATE GANACHE
4 oz unsweetened baking chocolate, chopped in small pieces
1/2 cup whipping cream
1/4 cup powdered sweetener (optional)
1 tbsp butter
1 tsp pure vanilla extract

Lisa Baker is a professional stand-up comedian and a poster child for how to rock a healthy way of life. I met Lisa years ago, but when she started on her journey to health, I got to know the remarkable person that stands behind the mic on that stage.

We watched from a distance as the love of her life, Brett, whisked her off her feet. As time went by, we heard how he held her hand, how he made her heart sing, and how much he made her laugh.

We knew the Lisa and Brett deal was sealed when he casually whipped up a healthier version of one of Lisa's favourite recipes: Nanaimo Cheesecake. Our Lisa was a goner.

Brett was gracious enough to give me the nod to tweak and play and make this recipe our own creation. We are grateful.

I'll give the final words to Lisa: "Unbutton pants, grab fork, and enjoy."

To prepare the pastry cream
1. Place the egg yolks in a medium bowl and whisk in the sweetener and salt until well combined. Set aside.
2. Place the whipping cream in a medium saucepan on a low-medium heat and bring it to a simmer. Do not boil. When it steams, reduce the heat to low. Slowly drizzle 1 cup of the hot cream into the yolks to temper them. If texture appears in the yolks, the cream is being added too fast. Slowly whisk the yolk/cream mixture back into the remaining cream in the saucepan and continue to whisk until thick and glossy, about 5 to 6 minutes. Remove from the heat and whisk in the butter and vanilla. Set aside to cool.

To prepare the crust
Melt the butter in a double boiler on a medium heat. Stir in the dry ingredients, and then slowly whisk in the egg. Whisk until the mixture thickens, then remove it from the heat. Stir in the coconut, nuts, and vanilla and allow the mixture to slightly cool. Press into a 9- by 9-inch pan. Refrigerate until firm.

To prepare the vanilla filling
Cream the butter and cream cheese until smooth. Whisk in the cooled pastry cream and sweetener. Spread the filling over the crust and refrigerate for at least 1 hour.

To prepare the chocolate ganache
1. Place the chocolate in a double boiler on a low heat and stir until melted. Whisk the whipping cream into the melted chocolate and cook until the ganache starts to steam. Do not allow it to boil. Remove from the heat and whisk in the sweetener, butter, and vanilla.
2. Allow to slightly cool, about 10 minutes. Then pour the ganache on the cake. Refrigerate.

NOTE: Do not make the ganache until after the cake has fully cooled.

Mixed Berry Crumble Squares

FOR THE BERRY FILLING

1/4 cup powdered sweetener

1/4 tsp xanthan gum

1 1/2 cup berries (partridgeberries, blueberries, and strawberries)

1/4 cup water

1/4 tsp salt

1/4 tsp nutmeg

FOR THE CREAM FILLING

12 oz cream cheese, at room temperature

1/2 cup powdered sweetener

1 tsp pure vanilla extract

pinch of salt

FOR THE CRUMBLE

3 1/2 cups almond flour

1 cup fine or medium unsweetened shredded coconut

1 cup powdered sweetener

2 tbsp coconut flour

1/4 tsp nutmeg

1/2 tsp salt

3/4 cup butter

2 tsp pure vanilla extract

This is one of our family faves that Nan used to make way back when, updated and tweaked into a healthy version. Now we get that just-like-Nan's taste, but without the blood glucose spike from the former ingredients.

These squares get tucked away in our freezer every winter in many different variations—we make them with all kinds of berries: bakeapples, blueberries, partridgeberries, blackberries ... sometimes even a combination of them all.

To prepare the berry filling

Whisk the xanthan gum into the sweetener and then combine with all the ingredients in a medium saucepan on a medium heat. As soon as the mixture starts to boil, reduce the heat to low, and simmer for 25 to 30 minutes, mashing and stirring as the berries cook. Continue to cook until the mixture has slightly thickened. Set aside to cool, then refrigerate.

To prepare the crumble

1. Preheat the oven to 350°F and prepare a 9- by 11-inch pan with parchment paper.
2. In a large bowl, whisk together all the dry ingredients, including the sweetener. Cream the butter and vanilla into the crumble mixture until fully combined. Press about half of the mixture firmly into the bottom of the pan. Bake for 10 minutes, then rotate and bake for another 10 to 12 minutes. Remove from the oven and set aside to cool.

To prepare the cream filling

Heat the cream cheese, in 1-inch cubes, in the microwave for 15 seconds on high. Whisk in the remaining cream ingredients.

To assemble

1. Spread the warm cream cheese mixture over the cooled crust. Refrigerate for about 30 minutes or until the cream cheese layer has chilled and firmed. When the cheese has cooled, stir the berries and spread the berry filling over the top.
2. Sprinkle the remaining crumbs on the top and then gently press them into the cream berry layer. Reduce the oven temperature to 325°F. Bake for 20 to 25 minutes, until the squares are golden on top and bottom. Let them cool slightly and then refrigerate to cool completely. Cut into squares only when they are completely cooled.

NOTE: Substitute the shredded coconut with an equal amount of almond flour for a shortbread-type base. Cooking time varies with the jam, depending on the berries' water content. The compote will thicken as it cools. For extra crumble topping, mix up a mini portion of crumbs to help cover the top properly.

DESSERT | 255

Peony and Pistachio Cake

FOR THE CANDIED PEONY PETALS
1 large egg white, whisked to a froth
15-20 organic red or dark pink peony petals
1/8 cup granulated sweetener

FOR THE CAKE
2 cups almond flour
1 cup powdered sweetener
1 1/2 tsp cream of tartar
1/2 tsp baking soda
1/4 tsp ground cardamom
1 cup shelled pistachios, finely ground, plus chopped pistachios for garnish
1 cup butter, at room temperature
4 large eggs
zest of 1 lemon
1 tbsp lemon juice
2 tbsp rosewater
1 tsp almond or pistachio extract

FOR THE CREAM
3/4 cup whipping cream
1/2 cup sour cream
2 tbsp powdered sweetener
1 tbsp rosewater

FOR THE SYRUP
1/4 cup lemon juice
1/3 cup rosewater
1/2 cup powdered sweetener
pinch of salt

Decadent, nutty, and slightly floral, this cake is a show-stopper. Be sure to use flowers from a clean garden with no pesticides. Roses or any edible flowers may be substituted for the peony petals. See the list of recommended edible flowers on page 266.

To prepare the candied peony petals
1. Preheat the oven to 170°F (or the oven's lowest setting) and line a baking sheet with parchment paper.
2. Use a small pastry brush to apply a thin coating of egg white on both sides of the petals, and then sprinkle sweetener on the egg white. Shake off any excess sweetener and place the petals on the prepared baking sheet.
3. Bake for 20 to 25 minutes until the petals have dried and are crispy.
4. Set aside to cool.

To make the cake
1. Increase the oven temperature to 325°F and line a 9-inch springform pan with parchment paper on the bottom and sides.
2. Combine all the dry ingredients, including the sweetener, in a large mixing bowl and slowly cream the butter into the dry mixture. Add the eggs, one at a time, then add the remaining cake ingredients. Transfer the batter to the prepared pan. Smooth the batter with an offset spatula and bake for 55 to 60 minutes or until the cake starts to pull away from the sides of the pan and a knife inserted in the centre of the cake comes out clean.
3. Do not remove the cake from the pan until it has completely cooled.
4. Drizzle the warm syrup on the cake as soon as it comes out of the oven.
5. Sprinkle the pistachios on the cake so that they adhere to the sticky top.

To prepare the syrup
1. Because the syrup must be warm, make it just before the cake comes out of the oven.
2. Combine all the syrup ingredients in a small saucepan on a medium heat. Whisk until it boils. Remove from the heat as soon as the syrup is warm and the sweetener has dissolved.
3. Transfer the cake to the refrigerator and cool completely before serving.

To prepare the cream
Whisk vigorously to combine all the cream ingredients until thickened, about 5 minutes. Refrigerate until needed.

To assemble
When ready to serve, pile the rose petals in the centre of the cake and serve with a spoonful of the cream.

DESSERT | 257

Roly Poly

FOR THE EGG WHITES
10 egg whites
1/2 tsp cream of tartar
1/2 cup powdered sweetener

FOR THE CAKE
1 cup almond flour
1 tbsp egg white powder
1/2 tsp cream of tartar
1/2 tsp baking soda
1/2 tsp xanthan gum
1/2 tsp espresso powder
1/4 cup cocoa
1/2 cup powdered sweetener
6 egg yolks

FOR THE FILLING
16 oz cream cheese, room temperature
1 tbsp lemon juice
1 cup powdered sweetener

1/2 cup raspberries, halved

Chocolate and raspberry are a classic pairing. They bring out the best in each other. The raspberry in this Swiss roll elevates the dessert and adds an element of freshness. And with the light fluffy chocolate cake, composed primarily of whipped egg whites, it's a match made in heaven.

This recipe uses more egg whites than it does yolks; it's always option to use a carton of egg whites in such situations. For best results, separate the eggs when they are cold, but allow to come to room temperature before making the whipped eggs for best results.

Add a sprinkling of powdered sweetener and a sprig of holly on top of the Roly Poly to turn this into a Christmas Yule Log fit for any table.

1. Preheat oven to 350°F and line a baking sheet with parchment paper. Remove eggs from the refrigerator and separate the yolks from the whites. Allow the egg to come to room temperature.
2. Using a stand or hand mixer, mix the egg white and cream of tartar. Start the mixer on low speed and slowly increase until the eggs are fully whipped. Add the sweetener and continue to mix on high until it is fully incorporated. Set aside.
3. Whisk all the dry ingredients together. Set aside.
4. Mix the egg yolks with the sweetener, then whisk into the dry mix. Add one-third of the whipped egg whites. It will take several minutes for the two elements to come together. Use a spatula to stir the second third of the egg white into the chocolate mix. Gently fold the last third of the egg whites in, taking care not to knock the air out of this final batter. Transfer to the prepared baking sheet and bake for 20 minutes.
5. Remove from the oven as set aside to cool. Do not refrigerate the cake.
6. When the cake has cooled to room temperature, cover the top with a full sheet of parchment and a cutting board or larger baking sheet and flip. Slowly peel the parchment paper from the cake.
7. Place the filling ingredients in a medium bowl and combine with a stand or hand mixer. Spread the filling on top of the cake and sprinkle the raspberries at one end. Using two hands, and starting at the end with the raspberries, slowly roll the iced cake into a tight cylinder. Be sure to leave the parchment on the baking sheet.
8. Wrap the roll firmly with plastic wrap so that the roll holds properly. Place it in the refrigerator for 8 hours or overnight.
9. Cut the Roly Poly into slices and serve.

Shortbread Cookies
❖ **WITH VARIATIONS**

2 cups almond flour
3/4 cup powdered sweetener
1/2 tsp salt
1/4 tsp xanthan gum
1/3 cup butter, at room temperature
2 tsp pure vanilla or almond extract

This recipe is such a joy to play with, but as you work the variations, expect … well, variations. All kitchens are different, all measuring spoons are slightly bigger or smaller, and the way we measure ingredients will differ. The composition of pans (metal, glass, ceramic, cast iron) bring varying results. Elevation and humidity will impact your end product.

You need to think on your feet in the kitchen and be reactive to changing conditions. It's a continual "When this happens, I do this. When that happens, I should do this instead." Never blindly follow any recipe.

Play with the variations, make the cookies bigger or smaller, and enjoy them in all forms.

1. Line a baking sheet with parchment paper.
2. Combine all the dry ingredients. Cream the butter into the dry mixture and combine thoroughly. Scoop out portions of dough and form into balls, about 1 to 1 1/2 ounces per cookie. Flatten each ball to about 1/3 inch thick and place on the prepared cookie sheet.
3. Refrigerate the sheet (with the formed cookies) for at least 1 hour or overnight. Cover with plastic wrap if it is being refrigerated overnight.
4. Preheat the oven to 350°F.
5. When the oven is hot, remove the baking sheet from the refrigerator and put it in the hot oven. Bake for 10 to 12 minutes or until golden, and let cool completely before removing the cookies from the pan. They will firm as they cool.

❖ **VARIATIONS**
Try adding one of the following variations to the basic recipe:
1/2 cup cherries, chopped and drained
1/2 cup chocolate chips, for a chocolatey twist
2 tbsp cocoa powder, for an extra chocolatey taste
1/4 cup dried cranberries, for a berry tang
2 tsp dried lavender, for a Provençal taste
Zest of 1 lemon, for a citrusy vibe
1/2 tsp Ceylon cinnamon or pumpkin pie spice, for a fall taste
1 tsp peppermint extract instead of vanilla, for a minty taste

Sour Cream Glazed Donuts

FOR THE DONUTS

1 1/2 cups almond flour
1 cup powdered sweetener
1/2 cup coconut flour
1 tsp cream of tartar
1/2 tsp baking soda
1/2 tsp nutmeg
1/4 tsp xanthan gum
1/4 tsp salt
1/3 cup butter, at room temperature
3 large eggs
3/4 cup sour cream
1 tsp pure vanilla extract

FOR THE SOUR CREAM GLAZE

3/4 cup sour cream
1/3 cup butter, at room temperature
1 tsp pure vanilla extract
3/4 cup powdered sweetener
1 tsp lemon juice

Nutmeg is the star of the show in this donut; it is the flavour hiding behind the taste of the old-fashioned donut. If it is removed from the recipe, this becomes just a regular donut, without pizazz.

Berries or other flavourings such as chocolate or cinnamon spices can be added to the batter.

To prepare the donuts
1. Preheat the oven to 350°F.
2. Grease a 12-hole donut pan with Baker's Magic (Pan) Release (page 273).
3. In a large mixing bowl, combine all the dry ingredients, including the sweetener, then cream in the butter. Then add the remaining ingredients and mix until fully incorporated.
4. Pipe the batter into the pans with a pastry bag (or a large freezer bag with the corner cut off). Fill to the edge of the pan so that each cavity is almost full.
5. Bake for 25 to 30 minutes, or until the donuts are fully cooked and a toothpick inserted in the centre comes out clean. Allow them to cool before removing them from the pan.

To prepare the sour cream glaze
1. Mix all the glaze ingredients in a medium saucepan on a low heat until a smooth liquid is obtained.
2. Dip the cooled donuts in the glaze. Either dip them in, top only, or fully submerge the donuts and scoop them out of the glaze with a fork or slotted spoon.
3. Drain on a cooling rack for about 1 minute and then transfer to a parchment-lined tray and refrigerate.

DESSERT | 263

Strawberry and Cream Mini Muffins

2 cups almond flour
1 cup powdered sweetener
2 tsp egg white powder
1 tsp cream of tartar
1/2 tsp baking soda
1/4 tsp xanthan gum
1/4 tsp salt
4 oz cream cheese, at room temperature
1/4 cup butter
2/3 cup diced strawberries
2 large eggs
1 tsp pure vanilla extract
1/3 cup whipping cream

These uber yummy strawberry and cream mini muffins are delightful as a quick-bite dessert or a grab-and-go breakfast.

What if you want to turn mini muffins into a loaf? Or maybe you've asked the opposite question: can you turn a cake or loaf recipe into cupcakes? It's all about surface area, and how much of the food is exposed to the heat of your oven.

By increasing the surface area and using the same amount of batter, the batter will be spread out more. When the batter is shallower, the centre will dry out faster. Adjust the recipe by decreasing the baking time and raising the temperature so that the outside will still brown in a shorter time. In this case, a quick hot oven will do the job.

Keep some of these in the freezer so you'll always have a little bit of special waiting for you.

1. Preheat the oven to 375°F. Grease a muffin pan.
2. Place all the dry ingredients, including the sweetener, in a large mixing bowl, and whisk until fully combined. Cream in the butter, cream cheese, and strawberries. Use a hand mixer to add the remaining ingredients, mixing between each addition. Fill each muffin cup about three-quarters full.
3. Bake for 12 to 15 minutes or until a toothpick inserted in the centre comes out clean. Let the pan sit for about 5 minutes before attempting to remove the muffins from the pan, then cool on a rack.

NOTE: It is best not to use muffin papers with mini muffins, as too much of the muffin is lost when the paper liner is removed.

For extra decadent mini muffins, fold in 1/4 cup diced (frozen) cream cheese after mixing with the hand mixer.

For regular sized muffins, reduce the oven temperature to 350°F and increase the baking time to 20 to 22 minutes.

For jumbo muffins, reduce the oven temperature to 325°F and increase the baking time to 25 to 28 minutes.

For a loaf or cake, decrease the oven temperature to 325°F and increase the baking time to approximately 45 to 60 minutes.

Always check baked items a few minutes before the suggested baking time. Some ovens run hot and, in this case, the muffins will need a shorter baking time.

Strawberry Shortcake Deconstructed

FOR THE MACERATED STRAWBERRIES
1 lb fresh strawberries, roughly chopped
2 tbsp lemon juice
1/4 cup powdered sweetener

FOR THE SHORTCAKES
1 cup almond flour
1/2 cup powdered sweetener
1/2 cup coconut flour
1 tbsp egg white powder
1/2 tsp cream of tartar
1/4 tsp baking soda
1/4 tsp xanthan gum
1/4 tsp nutmeg
1/4 tsp salt
1/4 cup butter, at room temperature
2 large eggs
1/4 cup sour cream
1 tsp pure vanilla extract

FOR THE CREAM
8 oz cream cheese, at room temperature
1/4 cup whipping cream
1 tsp pure vanilla extract
1/8 tsp salt

FOR THE GARNISH
2-3 basil leaves, chiffonaded or rolled together into a tight cylinder or cigar shape and then thinly sliced

Easy to make, yummy, and thoroughly satisfying.

I love fancy recipes—but my preference will always be to find the easiest and most fuss-free way to get something done. My mind just works that way; it's like it has its own little microprocessor that turns things inside out and translates to *simplify*.

That often means stepping away from *this is the way it must be done* and toward *let's try it this way instead*.

You can take the painstaking steps of assembling this recipe as a cake with perfect layers or you can do it rustic style as described here. If you know me, you know which way I will always choose.

Make sure to start macerating the berries ahead of time, the longer they sit in the sweetener and lemon juice the juicier they will be.

To prepare the macerated strawberries
Place all the ingredients in a medium glass bowl and toss to combine. Let the mixture sit at room temperature, tossing or stirring occasionally, while the shortcakes bake. The sweetener and the lemon juice will pull the liquid from the berries and create a syrup.

To prepare the shortcakes
1. Preheat the oven to 350°F and line a baking sheet with parchment paper.
2. Combine all the dry ingredients, including the sweetener, in a large mixing bowl. Cream the butter into the dry mixture and then add all the remaining ingredients and mix well with a whisk.
3. Mould the mixture into 6 individual shortcakes and bake for 5 minutes, and then reduce the oven temperature to 325°F to allow the insides of the shortcakes to cook through. Cook at the reduced temperature for an additional 15 to 20 minutes or until the edges start to brown.
4. Let the shortcakes cool for at least 15 minutes.
5. Gently halve the shortcakes by hand for a rustic look or cut them with a knife for a more refined look. Plate the bottom shortcake halves, followed by a dollop of cream, then the macerated strawberries. Cover with the top shortcake halves.
6. Drizzle any syrupy juices left in the bowl on the top and garnish with the basil ribbons.

Walnut Ginger Carrot Cake
❖ **VARIATION: CHOCOLATE CARROT LOAF**

A light and lofty ginger-flavoured carrot cake that will redefine how you think about carrot cake. It can be made without the accoutrements as a plain carrot cake.

Make your own candied ginger; store-bought candied ginger contains more sugar than ginger. This allows you to control how much and what kind of sweetener to use. Make the ginger ahead of time and freeze it.

FOR THE CAKE
2 cups almond flour
2 tsp egg white powder
1 1/2 tsp cream of tartar
1/2 tsp baking soda
2 tsp ground ginger
1 tsp Ceylon cinnamon
1/4 tsp nutmeg
1/2 tsp salt
3/4 cup powdered sweetener
1/4 cup butter
3 large eggs, at room temperature
1/4 cup oil
1/4 cup whipping cream
1 tsp pure vanilla extract
1 1/2 cups coarsely grated carrots
1/2 cup chopped walnut pieces (optional)
1/2 cup finely chopped crystallized ginger (optional)

FOR THE ICING
1 cup butter, at room temperature
1 cup powdered sweetener
8 oz cream cheese, at room temperature
1 tbsp coarsely grated fresh ginger
pinch of salt

FOR THE CANDIED GINGER (OPTIONAL)
6-inch knob of ginger, peeled and cut in 1/2-inch pieces
3 cups water
3/4 cup powdered sweetener
1/4 cup apple cider or white vinegar
1/4 tsp salt

To prepare the candied ginger
1. Place the ginger in a pot of cold water and bring the water to a boil. Boil for 30 minutes. Drain and rinse. Repeat this process twice. Add the sweetener and enough fresh water to cover the ginger and boil. Do not rinse or drain this time. Reduce and again add enough water to cover; repeat until the ginger starts to turn from white and opaque to translucent.
2. Add the vinegar and salt and continue to boil for about 20 to 25 minutes. Allow the water to boil off this time, reducing the heat as the pan dries. Watch carefully at this stage.
3. Remove the pot from the heat and place the ginger in a dehydrator or an oven at its lowest temperature setting until it has fully dried. Place it in an airtight container and then the freezer.

To prepare the cake
1. Preheat the oven to 350°F and line a 9-inch springform pan with parchment paper.
2. Combine all the dry ingredients, including the sweetener, in a large mixing bowl. Cream in the butter and beat in the wet ingredients, including the walnuts, carrot, and ginger, until everything is completely combined. Use a rubber spatula to scrape the batter into the prepared pan and smooth the top.
3. Bake for 45 to 55 minutes or until golden brown and the cake pulls away from the edges of the pan and a knife inserted in the centre of the cake comes out with just a few crumbs stuck to it. Allow the cake to cool for about 25 minutes before removing it from the pan. Set aside to cool completely.

To prepare the icing
Combine all the ingredients and beat on high until the icing is completely smooth. Spread the icing on the cake and then sprinkle with chopped walnuts and candied ginger if desired.

❖ **VARIATION: CHOCOLATE CARROT LOAF**
You know me—I have to keep going and tweaking. And now: the ooey gooey decadent chocolate version of my carrot cake. The consistency of this reminds me of a high-quality dark fruitcake ... only chocolate and without the fruit. Remove the walnut, ginger, and cinnamon from the recipe above and replace with 1/3 cup cocoa powder, 1 teaspoon espresso powder or instant coffee, 1 cup chocolate chips (try 1/2 unsweetened, 1/2 milk chocolate). For the sweetener, try 1/4 cup brown sweetener and 3/4 cup powdered white sweetener. Follow the instructions above.

Extras and Sauces

Extras! Extras! Read All about It ...

Bacon Mayonnaise
Baker's Magic (Pan) Release
Blackberry Grill Sauce
Cheese Ball
Cocktail Sauce
Donair Meat and Sweet Sauce
Eggnog
Figgy(less) Pudding
Honey Mustard Glaze
Jakey Buns (Tea Biscuits)
Maple Syrup Substitute
Marshmallow
Mustard Vinaigrette Dressing
Peanut Butter Granola
Protein Pizza Crust—Margherita Pizza
Soured Dough Bread
Spinach Dip
Tartar Sauce
Teriyaki Sauce
White Chocolate

Many of us don't take time to think about condiments and sauces—we grab a bottle off the shelf and go the easy route. But tartar sauce, mayo, and BBQ sauces are all super easy to make.

We are used to a generic form of all these extras. Something mass-produced to fit the tastes of many not necessarily the best representation of what these food items are meant to be. When tasting anything new, there is a learning curve. You need to give your palate a little time to adjust.

These extras are the very things we should be going out of our way to make at home. They're so much tastier and creamier than the store-bought stuff. It's what gives the pizza the pizzazz, it's what puts the spice in Caesar dressing, and what makes all our sides (and life) a little saucier. Once you dive in and start making your own, there's no going back.

No need to call the news media, just go ahead and reach for a little homemade extra ... starting with these fab recipes.

Bacon Mayonnaise

❖ **VARIATION: SPICY BACONNAISE**

1 large egg
1 tbsp lemon juice
1 tbsp white wine vinegar
1 tsp Dijon mustard
1/2 tsp salt, or to taste
1/4 tsp pepper, or to taste
1/2 cup oil
1/2 cup bacon grease, warmed

I like spicy food, but Geoff craves uber spicy food. I often have tears running out of my eyes when he says, "It's not very spicy, is it?" Geoff's right amount of heat is usually burn-your-face-off level to most of the outside world.

Based on this, we usually have two bottles of this mayo in our refridgerator, one that has no labelling at all and one with a big S on it to advise that super spicy things are lurking inside.

We use this mayo on eggs, on our French fries as a replacement for ketchup, or even as a dip for wings, beef, or pork. The possibilities are endless.

This recipe and its variation can be tailor-made to your own spice needs.

1. Place all the ingredients except the bacon grease in a long narrow vessel, such as an immersion blender container, allowing the egg to sink to the bottom. Mix all the ingredients with an immersion blender, starting with the blender at the bottom and slowly moving to the top. The mayonnaise texture changes as the blender moves to the top. Slowly drizzle in the warm bacon grease while blending.
2. Chill and serve.

NOTE: Right out of the blender, the mayonnaise will be runny. If it is left at room temperature, it will harden slightly. When it is refrigerated, it will harden to the consistency of butter. Use a neutral tasting or light oil, or the mayonnaise will taste too strong.

❖ **VARIATION: SPICY BACON-NAISE**

Add 2 tablespoons hot or chili garlic sauce to taste. If you are buying commercially made sauces, choose those with no starches or additives—look for those with the smallest and simplest ingredients list.

Want a basic mayonnaise? Add 1 cup oil (try 1/2 olive oil and 1/2 unflavoured [liquid] coconut or avocado), 2 teaspoons Dijon mustard, 1 teaspoon apple cider vinegar, 1 teaspoon lemon juice, and 1/4 to 1/2 teaspoon salt, and mix with an immersion blender. Add 1 large egg yolk, allowing it to settle to the bottom. Starting at the bottom of the vessel, blend upward, slowly moving to the top.

Baker's Magic (Pan) Release

1/2 cup lard, at room temperature
1/2 cup olive oil
1/4 cup coconut flour

I was late to the pan release party. A colleague casually mentioned goop he was using to unstick his pans. I dismissed the idea at the time—we didn't use grain flour or shortening in our recipes.

The dawning happened after I struggles to create a cake in a pretty Bundt pan—no matter what I tried, the cake stuck to the pan.

A new version came to me in the wee hours of the morning. It worked like a charm and is my new favourite thing in the kitchen.

Place all the ingredients in a medium mixing bowl and mix well with a hand mixer until fully incorporated and fluffy. Store in airtight glass bottles on the countertop or in a pantry. When ready to use, brush on a thin layer with a pastry brush. Do not apply a thick layer as it can goop up and cause baked goods to stick.

Blackberry Grill Sauce

4 cups fresh blackberries
1 cup chicken or vegetable broth
1 cup powdered sweetener
1/2 cup apple cider or white vinegar
2 tbsp fresh ginger, grated
1 tbsp smoked paprika
1 tbsp garlic powder
2 tsp chili powder
1 1/2 tsp salt
1 tsp dried basil
1/2 tsp pepper
1/4 tsp nutmeg
1/4 tsp ground cardamom
1/4 tsp ground sage
1/4 cup oil, to finish

BBQ sauce doesn't have to be tomato based! You will love this on chicken and love it even more on pork.

We love this sauce so much we've made it a priority to source frozen blackberries to make this delicious sauce even more affordable than using fresh berries. We have a bunch of bags of frozen berries to set ourselves up for fast action whenever we want to make a batch.

1. Place all the ingredients in a medium saucepan on a medium-high heat. When the sauce bubbles, reduce the heat to low and simmer. Mash the blackberries well as they cook.
2. Let the blackberry mixture cool slightly and then press it through a fine mesh colander or use a vegetable mill to remove the seeds.
3. Return the sauce to the saucepan and simmer on a medium heat to reduce to desired thickness.
4. Drizzle in the oil while whisking to make the sauce glossy and give it a finished look.

Cheese Ball

▶ **EXTRA: BLUE CHEESE BALL**

8 oz cream cheese, at room temperature

1/2 cup sour cream

8 oz grated cheddar cheese

8 oz grated mozzarella or Swiss cheese

6 strips bacon, cooked and crumbled

1/4 cup minced bell pepper or jalapeño pepper

2 green onions, minced

1 tbsp fish sauce

1 tsp garlic powder

1/2 tsp onion powder

1/2 tsp dried onion flakes

1/2 tsp pepper

1/4 tsp nutmeg

1 cup roasted and chopped pecans

You've got company coming! The crackers are baking, the veggies are chopped, pork rinds are ready. Now, what do you scoop up? Cheese ball to the rescue!

Creamy cheesy and herb filling with a pecan coating come together to bring a delicious centrepiece to any gathering.

1. Combine all the ingredients except the pecans and form into a ball. Roll the ball in the pecan pieces and place the ball in the centre of a sheet of plastic wrap. Seal and refrigerate it for at least 1 hour to firm up.
2. Serve with a choice of crackers/bread, pork rinds, vegetable sticks, and other charcuterie items.

▶ **BLUE CHEESE BALL**

Add 4 ounces blue cheese for a tangy and tart variation. Or add 1/4 cup chopped fresh herbs, such as a combination of parsley, thyme, oregano, and basil.

Cocktail Sauce

1/2 cup tomato sauce

1 tsp powdered sweetener

1 tbsp prepared horseradish

1 tsp lemon juice

1/2 tsp lemon zest

1 tsp fish sauce

1 tsp chili sauce

1/2 tsp onion powder

1 tsp garlic powder

1/2 tsp salt

1/4 tsp pepper

1 tsp Tabasco (optional)

Most commercially available cocktail sauces are loaded with sugars and starches. Fortunately, it's easy to make your own.

Combine all the ingredients and refrigerate for 10 minutes before using.

NOTE: Do not omit the horseradish, as it gives cocktail sauce its distinctive flavour.

Donair Meat and Sweet Sauce

FOR THE MEAT
3 tsp garlic powder
1 1/2 tsp fennel seed, crushed
1 tsp salt
1 tsp coconut flour
1 tsp onion powder
1 tsp paprika
1 tsp pepper
1 tsp dried oregano
1/2 tsp dried basil
1/2 tsp dried thyme
1/4 tsp ground rosemary
1/2 tsp Korean chili flakes
1 lb medium ground beef
1/2 lb ground pork

FOR THE SAUCE
3/4 cup whipping cream
1/4 cup powdered sweetener
1/4 cup oil
4 garlic cloves
1/2 tsp salt
1/2 tsp pepper
3 tbsp white vinegar
1 tsp Dijon mustard
1 large egg yolk

In the 1950s, Peter Gamoulakos, a Greek immigrant in Halifax, adapted his gyro recipe to better suit the Canadian market: the result was the donair.

This donair meat can be eaten straight from the oven, but to enjoy it as it was intended, it should be slightly cooled, cut into thick slabs, and fried until the outsides are brown and crispy. The sweet garlic sauce is essential to the full experience.

To prepare the donair meat
1. Mix the spices together in a small mixing bowl and then sprinkle this mixture on the meat. Work the spices through it, kneading firmly. To achieve a smooth texture and to hold it together when sliced, the meat must be compressed thoroughly and forcefully. Throw it down with force onto the countertop or workspace about 20 to 25 times, kneading it after each throw.
2. Form the finished meat into thin loaves and wrap in plastic wrap. Wrap in a cylinder and twist the ends to further compress the loaf, and then refrigerate it overnight, if possible.
3. Preheat the oven to 350°F and line a baking sheet with parchment paper.
4. Remove the meat from the plastic wrap and bake for 30 minutes, placing a bowl of water in the oven to keep the meat moist. Flip the loaf and continue to roast for another 45 minutes. Remove from the oven and cool.

To prepare the sauce
In a medium saucepan on a low heat, combine all the ingredients except the vinegar. Cook 10 to 15 minutes or until the sauce reaches the desired consistency. Add the vinegar in portions, tasting until the perfect level of acidity is achieved. Refrigerate the sauce until serving.

To assemble
1. Slice the meatloaf into 1/4-inch-thick slices and cook them in a sauté pan on a medium heat until both sides are brown and crisp, about 5 minutes per side.
2. Serve with chopped onion and tomatoes on a lettuce leaf or choice of wrap.

NOTE: Use a food processor to finely grind the beef, pulse in the remaining ingredients, then mix by hand so that it is thoroughly combined. For a more authentic taste, substitute one-quarter of the beef with lamb. Try this with Caesar dressing (page 137) instead of the sweet garlic sauce.

Eggnog

6 large egg yolks
1/2 cup powdered sweetener
2 cups whipping cream
1 cup water
1 tsp freshly grated nutmeg
1/2 tsp Ceylon cinnamon
2 tsp pure vanilla extract
1 cup whiskey, rum, or brandy,
   or 2 tbsp rum extract (optional)

This eggnog is Christmas in a cup. Add a little Christmas cheer or drink it alcohol-free; it's lovely either way.

1. In a large bowl, whisk the egg yolks with the sweetener until fully combined. Set aside.
2. Place the cream, water, and spices in a medium saucepan on a low heat, and stir until it steams. Do not boil. Slowly, while whisking, drizzle 1 cup of the hot cream mixture into the egg yolks to temper the eggs. Whisk the tempered yolks back into the cream. Return the mixture to the saucepan and cook on a low-medium heat until the eggnog is slightly thick and coats the back of a spoon. Remove from the heat and stir in the extracts and, if using, the whiskey. Refrigerate until chilled.
3. Garnish with whipped cream and a sprinkle of cinnamon.

Figgy(less) Pudding

1 cup almond flour
1/3 cup coconut flour
1 cup powdered sweetener
1 1/2 tsp cream of tartar
1 tsp baking soda
2 tsp Ceylon cinnamon
1 tsp ground ginger
1 tsp cocoa powder
1/2 tsp allspice
1/2 tsp ground cardamom
1/4 tsp xanthan gum
1/3 cup butter, at room temperature
1/4 cup tomato sauce
1/2 cup finely shredded carrots
2 large eggs
3/4 cup whipping cream
2 tsp pure vanilla extract

Make sure that this pudding is steamed and does not come in contact with the water at any time. It can be served on the dinner plate as part of the main or as dessert, topped with rum and butter sauce (page 242), cream cheese sauce, or caramel sauce. Use a steamer or a traditional pudding bag.

1. Whisk together all the dry ingredients, including the sweetener, in a medium mixing bowl.
2. Using a hand or stand mixer, mix all the wet ingredients together in a large bowl.
3. Combine the wet and dry ingredients in one bowl.
4. Transfer the batter to a pudding steamer, leaving room for expansion.
5. Bring a pot of water to a boil and steam the pudding for approximately 1 1/2 hours.

Top this pudding with English toffee sauce
1/4 cup butter
1/2 cup powdered sweetener
1/4 tbsp whipping cream
1 tsp pure vanilla or toffee extract

Combine all the ingredients except the vanilla in a medium saucepan on a low heat. Stir until the toffee turns to a dark amber and thickens. Remove from the heat, stir in the vanilla, and allow to cool.

NOTE: Avoid raisins, which are high in natural sugars, but 1/2 cup partridgeberries or blueberries may be added to the pudding. If the pudding is to be served with a traditional boiled dinner, use a traditional pudding bag. In this case, wet the pudding bag and fill it to three-quarters full. Tie off the top of the bag with kitchen string and then place it in the pot so that it sits on the vegetables. The pudding bag should not touch the water.

Honey Mustard Glaze

1/3 cup brown sweetener
1/4 cup Dijon mustard
1/4 cup yellow mustard
2 tbsp whole-grain mustard (optional)
1 tsp dried parsley
1 tsp garlic powder
1 tsp salt (optional)
1/2 tsp pepper
1/2 tsp dried thyme

This sweet and tangy sauce tastes great with ham, chicken, or salmon and is super easy to make. Do not add the optional salt if using this glaze on ham, as the ham will be salty enough. Cook the ham without the glaze. When it has cooked, pull off chunks and cover those with glaze and bake. This gives the option to reserve unglazed ham for breakfast and glazed for an evening meal.

Mix all the ingredients together in a small mixing bowl and spoon the glaze on the ham (or choice of protein) before cooking.

NOTE: Omit the salt if using this glaze for a ham.

Jakey Buns (Tea Biscuits)

1 cup plus 2 tbsp almond flour
1/4 cup powdered sweetener
1/4 cup coconut flour
1/2 tsp salt
1/2 tsp cream of tartar
1/4 tsp baking soda
1/4 tsp xanthan gum
1/4 cup butter
2 large eggs
1/4 cup sour cream

The rest of the world calls them tea biscuits, but I know them as Jakey buns.

This recipe originated with my grandmother. Nan would tell of a visitor (maybe the visitor was Jakey, who knows?) who arrived while she was baking these buns.

"Do you want a bun?" Nan asked the visitor.

The response was always the same. "Do I want a bun," he says. "Do I want a bun? More like, do I want a dozen of the little things?"

Don't be like Jakey and eat a dozen, even if they are that good. One at a time, please.

1. Preheat the oven to 350°F and line a baking sheet with parchment paper.
2. Combine all the dry ingredients, including the sweetener, together. Cream in the butter, and then mix in the eggs and sour cream, being careful not to overmix the batter. Use the extra almond flour if the batter is not thick enough to mould. Mould the mixture into a flat disc and use a metal cutter or a small glass to cut round biscuits or form them by hand.
3. Place the biscuits on the prepared pan and bake for 20 to 25 minutes or until the edges start to turn golden brown.

Maple Syrup Substitute

1/2 cup powdered sweetener
1/2 tsp xanthan gum
1/4 tsp salt
1/4 cup butter
1 cup water
1 tsp pure vanilla extract
1 tbsp maple extract

Our maple syrup substitute is an easy addition to any plate of pancakes, waffles or even in situations where you would add maple flavour to a recipe, as in our maple garlic BBQ sauce page 177.

This sauce can be made without the maple extract if you're in need of a quick sweet sauce but don't have the extract in your pantry.

1. Whisk all the dry ingredients together.
2. Place the butter in a medium sauté pan on a low heat and heat until it turns a golden brown. Swirl the pan as the butter cooks to ensure that it does not scorch. Whisk in the sweetener and then the water. Continue to cook until the syrup reaches the desired consistency.
3. Stir in the extracts after the syrup has been taken off the heat.

Marshmallow

- 1 cup water, divided
- 3 tbsp unflavoured gelatin
- 1 3/4 cups allulose or another powdered sweetener
- 1/4 tsp salt
- 1 tsp pure lemon extract
- 3-4 drops natural yellow food colouring
- 1/3 cup powdered sweetener, to dust (optional)

The hardest part of making marshmallows was sticking to the packet directions for the gelatin. I wanted to take that product and make it work in another manner. I wanted to Bobbi-ize it! There are not enough letters in the word fail to express how many times my attempts failed.

Success was found when I followed those instructions and used the product as it was intended with the other ingredients..

1. Line a 9- by 9-inch baking dish with parchment paper and apply a thin coating of oil. Set aside.
2. Place 1/2 cup warm water in a stand mixer bowl. Sprinkle the gelatin into the water and let it bloom while making the sweetener mixture.
3. Place the allulose, 1/2 cup water, and salt in a medium saucepan. Bring to a boil on a medium heat. Cook until the mixture reaches a temperature of 240° to 245°F. As the allulose mixture reaches the desired temperature, turn the mixer to a low speed to mix the bloomed gelatin. Slowly pour the hot allulose mixture into the gelatin mixture about 1 inch into the bowl (not on the edge or the middle) and continue at a low speed for about 1 minute. Increase the speed to high for 10 to 15 minutes.
4. When the mixture reaches the stiff peak stage, add the extract and colouring and mix for 1 more minute on high to fully incorporate.
5. Transfer the mixture to the prepared pan and spread it out as quickly as possible. It sets fast.
6. Set aside for about 6 to 8 hours to dry out.
7. When set, cut the marshmallows into squares and separate them to allow the pieces to continue to dry out.
8. Dust the dried pieces with powdered sweetener, if desired.
9. Refrigerate in an airtight container.

NOTE: If using a hand mixer, use a large glass or metal bowl. Allulose is recommended for this recipe; other sweeteners can be used but the results may vary. Natural yellow food colouring and lemon extract can be swapped out to accommodate other flavours and colours.

Mustard Vinaigrette Dressing

- 1/4 cup Dijon mustard
- 3/4 cup olive oil
- 2/3 cup chopped green onions
- 1/4 cup white vinegar
- 1 clove garlic minced, or 1 tsp garlic powder
- 1 tbsp dried parsley, or a handful of fresh parsley
- 1 tbsp powdered sweetener
- 2 tsp dried sage or tarragon
- 1 tsp salt, or to taste
- 1/2 tsp pepper, or to taste
- 1/2 tsp Korean chili flakes (optional)

A vibrant salad dressing for a green salad with origins in French cooking. Try this versatile dressing as a dipping sauce or marinade for meats.

Combine all the ingredients and drizzle on any green salad.

NOTE: For extra zip, add a few dashes of hot sauce.

Peanut Butter Granola

❖ **VARIATION: GRANOLA BARS**

1 1/2 cups chopped pecans
1 cup medium unsweetened coconut
1/2 cup sliced almonds
1/2 cup pine nuts
1/2 cup sunflower seeds
1/2 cup pumpkin seeds
1/2 cup shelled pistachios
1/2 cup flax meal
2 tsp pure vanilla or maple extract
1/2 cup egg white powder
1/2 cup butter, melted
1 cup powdered sweetener (try 3/4 cup white and 1/4 cup brown sweetener)
3 large eggs
1 tsp Ceylon cinnamon
1/2 tsp ground cardamom
1/2 tsp salt
1 cup natural peanut or almond butter

At first glance, this may seem like a hard recipe based on the number of ingredients, but once you have everything on hand, it's an easy dump in the mixing bowl and then onto a sheet tray.

Instead of peanut butter, use almond butter for a milder taste. Any nuts or seeds may be substituted in this recipe, but some are higher in carbs than others.

1. Preheat the oven to 275°F and line a baking sheet with parchment paper.
2. Place all the ingredients in a large mixing bowl and stir to combine. Spoon the mixture on the prepared baking sheet. Bake for 10 minutes, then remove and stir. Bake for another 5 minutes for a softer granola or another 5 to 10 minutes for a crispy granola. The granola will crisp up as it cools.
3. Refrigerate uncovered overnight or for 12 hours.

NOTE: Add chocolate (1/4 cup cocoa powder) before baking for a peanut butter chocolate granola. Add chocolate chips when the granola has slightly cooled, or they will melt. Visit a bulk store to purchase only the quantity of nuts and seeds needed for this recipe and avoid buying big bags that will sit in the pantry forever.

❖ **VARIATION: GRANOLA BARS**
Add 1 extra, large egg and firmly press the granola mix on a parchment-paper-lined baking sheet and bake for 12 to 15 minutes. Let cool completely in the refrigerator and cut in squares.

Want more flavour variations? Try the following variations

Cranberry almond
Lemon blueberry
Pumpkin
Mint

Bacon
Ginger blackberry
Chai spice
Plain vanilla or chocolate

EXTRAS AND SAUCES | 287

Protein Pizza Crust – Margherita Pizza

FOR THE CRUST
16 oz grated mozzarella cheese
1 tsp garlic powder
1/2 tsp dried oregano
1/2 tsp onion powder
1/2 tsp xanthan gum
1/4 tsp dried basil
1 cup powdered pork panko (crushed pork rinds), or 1 cup ground pork/chicken, or 1 can (flakes, not chunks) chicken
2 large eggs

FOR THE TOPPINGS
2 tbsp tomato sauce and/or 1 medium Roma tomato, thinly sliced and slightly dried with a paper towel
fresh buffalo mozzarella cheese, cut in 1-inch pieces
salt and pepper, or to taste

oil, to finish
8-10 fresh basil leaves, to finish

This recipe includes several protein options. The canned and fresh chicken version was my favourite; the fresh pork and crushed pork rinds seemed to overpower the taste of the crust for my liking. Geoff, on the other hand, enjoyed the crushed pork rind option best of all and said it felt like meat-za to the extreme.

This crust is great for those who are in pursuit of zero carb, or for those who don't do well with almond flour. In addition to tasting like a traditional crust, it's gluten-free and diabetic-friendly.

To prepare the crust
1. Preheat the oven to 350°F.
2. Tear off two pieces (a little bigger than the crust) of parchment paper.
3. In a large bowl, combine the spices with the cheese. When fully combined, add the meat, and knead in the egg. Place the dough between the two pieces of parchment paper and use a rolling pin to roll out the dough, or mould the edges of the dough by hand.
4. Bake the crust for 10 minutes, then flip by gripping the double sheets of parchment. Bake for another 10 to 12 minutes. The crust is ready.

To assemble
1. Spread a thin layer of tomato sauce on the pizza (if too thick, the crust will be soggy). Place the tomato slices around the outside edge of the crust and then continue laying them out in a circular fashion in the centre of the pizza.
2. Place the mozzarella pieces around the pizza crust, keeping them about 1 inch from the outside edge so that the cheese does not melt off the pizza. Season with the salt and pepper, then bake for 10 to 15 minutes until the cheese is melted and the toppings are warm.
3. Remove the pizza from the oven and allow it to cool slightly. Place the basil leaves on the pizza and finish with a drizzle of good-quality olive oil. Cut in slices.

Pizza combinations
Steak and onion
BBQ sauce and chicken
Butter chicken
Tex Mex

Caramelized onion and feta
Breakfast pizza
Spinach and goat cheese
Roasted vegetables

NOTE: Mince the ground pork or chicken in a blender to achieve a fine mince. Powder pork rinds in a blender or mini blender after crushing them to ensure very small pieces. Prebake the ground and canned meat for 20 to 25 minutes at 350°F to dry out the protein before adding it to the crust. If not, the crust may be soggy. More than five toppings make the pizza too heavy. Choose unprocessed meats and fresh vegetables where possible. As the crust contains mostly cheese, it is not needed on top unless an alternate cheese such as buffalo mozzarella or feta cheese is being used.

Soured Dough Bread

FOR THE BREAD

1/3 cup psyllium husk
2 tbsp flax meal
2 tbsp nutritional yeast
1 1/2 cups almond flour
1/2 cup coconut flour
2 tsp cream of tartar
1 tsp powdered sweetener
1/2 tsp salt
1/2 tsp xanthan gum
1 tsp baking soda
6 large egg whites, or 1 cup egg whites
1/4 cup whipping cream
1 tbsp lemon juice
2 tbsp apple cider vinegar
1/2 cup hot water

FOR DUSTING

2 tbsp almond flour
1 tbsp coconut flour

Many of my recipes are fuelled by memories, most often of family and of times gone by. This recipe will always remind me of my father. Dad appreciates my time spent in the kitchen, even more so after losing my mother, as he now finds himself in his own kitchen and making meals.

On the day in question, I had made him a simple grilled cheese sandwich. I could tell that he was really enjoying it, but I was moved by his words: "My, oh my," he said. "That bread in this grilled cheese is some good. It takes me right back to a little diner where I used to get a grilled cheese as a boy. That was 60 years ago, but for a second, I was right back there."

There was a twinkle in his eye as he told me. I was sure it was a mote of memory welling up in his heart as he reminisced.

I was glad to have the opportunity to walk down memory lane with Dad into his past. His memory has now become a part of my food memory. How awesome is that!

1. Place the psyllium husk, flax meal, and nutritional yeast in a blender or mini blender and pulse to a fine powder. Then combine all the dry ingredients in a large bowl and set aside.
2. Combine the wet ingredients, except the water, in a medium bowl.
3. Preheat the oven to 350°F. Line a baking sheet or a covered baking dish with parchment paper. Set aside.
4. Use a light hand and a spatula or a broad wooden spoon to fold the wet ingredients (not the water) into the dry ingredients. Add the water in increments until the dough is workable. Sprinkle some of the dusting powder on a work surface and gently knead the dough into a loaf. Transfer the loaf to the baking sheet or dish and dust with the remaining flour. Using a lame or sharp knife, carve a design about 1/4- to 1/2-inch deep. Make one bigger single slash to promote expansion in the loaf, and add smaller delicate cuts to create a more intricate design.
5. Set the loaf in a warm place to rest for 15 minutes before baking. This lightens the loaf and marries the flavours.
6. Cover with a lid or aluminum foil so that the dusting flour will not scorch.
7. Bake for 15 minutes covered, then reduce the heat to 300°F and bake the loaf (still covered) for 40 to 50 minutes. Then uncover and bake for another 15 to 25 minutes to crisp up the crust.
8. If not dusting and carving, follow the same temperature and times, without covering.

NOTE: A dough hook on low speed can be used to knead the dough.

Never add all the wet ingredients to a batter right away. Work in increments.

In this recipe, vinegar and lemon juice sours the cream. A traditional sourdough starter would not be considered keto.

This bread will have a darker crust and look done before it is fully baked. Patience is needed with this recipe. Let it cook.

Various psyllium husk brands affect this recipe in different ways, and some even tint it purple. This is often a chemical reaction between excess heat, psyllium, and baking soda and it does not mean that the taste is compromised.

Elevate this recipe

Try adding garlic and Italian herbs. Mix 1 teaspoon each dried parsley and garlic powder, 1/2 teaspoon each dried oregano and dried basil, and 1/4 teaspoon dried thyme and dried rosemary. Add to the dry ingredients for an Italian loaf. For buns, reduce the baking time to 25 to 30 minutes.

Take caution

Psyllium husk absorbs water and can cause dehydration. Eat this (and any other recipe with psyllium husk) in moderation and increase water intake. Do not over-hydrate; instead, listen to your body and quench your thirst on demand.

Spinach Dip

3 cups fresh spinach, or 10 oz frozen spinach
8 oz cream cheese
3/4 cup sour cream
12 oz grated mozzarella cheese
10 oz grated Parmesan cheese
1 tsp dried parsley
1 tsp dried chives
1 tsp dried oregano
1 tsp salt
1/2 tsp pepper
1/2 tsp chili powder
2 tsp garlic powder, or 4 cloves garlic, minced
1 tbsp onion powder or flakes
1/2 tsp fish sauce
1/2 tsp Dijon mustard

OPTIONAL INGREDIENTS

1/2 cup cooked and crumbled bacon
1/4 cup diced sun-dried tomatoes
1/2 cup diced mushrooms, cooked

This recipe was created for my daughter-in-law, Kayla. She's a big fan of spinach dip and I wanted to give her a dip that she and son-of-mine can make together in their kitchen. Nothing pleases me more than knowing my kids (and other loved ones) are loving and laughing while creating in the hearth of the home.

You can make this dip with either fresh or frozen spinach, but fresh will always be nicer. Make sure you squeeze all the water out of the spinach for a better consistency.

1. Pan-wilt fresh spinach, or thaw frozen spinach. Drain the spinach extremely well and roughly chop it. Combine the spinach and cream cheese in a large mixing bowl. Add the remaining ingredients, reserving half of the mozzarella cheese. Mix well to fully incorporate.
2. Scoop the dip into an oven-safe baking dish, sprinkle the reserved cheese on top, and bake at 350°F until golden, about 18 or 30 minutes. Let cool slightly (cheese will be molten) and serve.

NOTE: The spinach should be measured before it is wilted.

Tartar Sauce

1 cup Mayonnaise (page 273)
1/4 cup dill pickles, finely chopped
2 tbsp minced shallots, or 1 tbsp chopped chives
1 tbsp lemon juice
1 tbsp fresh dill (optional)
1/2 tsp salt
1/4 tsp pepper, or to taste
a few sprigs of parsley

A quick and easy tartar sauce for seafood feasts.

The flavour profile for this sauce can be changed up to suit your own tastes; add the optional capers for a salty/briny tang or try it with Dijon, tarragon, fish sauce, or hot sauce.

Mix all the ingredients and set aside to chill.

NOTE: Add 1 tablespoon capers for an extra briny tartar sauce.

Teriyaki Sauce

5 cloves garlic, minced and salted
2 tbsp oil
1/2 cup powdered sweetener
1/4 cup coconut sauce
1/3 cup water
2 tsp grated fresh ginger
1 tsp fish sauce
1 tsp salt
1/2 tsp pepper

A saucy all-star player to suit any occasion. We love pairing this sauce with salmon and chicken, but any meat will work.

Add this sauce in the final 10 minutes of cooking; if you add it before then, the sweeteners may scorch before the meat is cooked.

Try this on roasted or grilled veggies.

1. Combine all the ingredients in a medium saucepan and simmer for 20 minutes.
2. Let cool, purée with an immersion blender, and then reduce to the desired consistency.

NOTE: To thicken the sauce, add 1/4 teaspoon xanthan gum.

White Chocolate

❖ **VARIATION: WHITE CHOCOLATE BARK**

- 1/3 cup heavy cream powder
- 1/4 cup powdered allulose
- 1/8 tsp sunflower lecithin
- 1/8 tsp salt
- 3 oz cacao butter, chopped in 1/2-inch or smaller pieces
- 2 tbsp refined liquid coconut oil
- 1 tsp pure vanilla extract

The younger version of myself would not have approved of this recipe. To my unrefined and youthful palate, there was no such thing as white chocolate. I'd even go so far as to say I wasn't even a believer in dark chocolate; I mean, what's the sense? Chocolate should be milk chocolate. Case closed!

The more mature me loves chocolate in all forms, and that includes the many different variations that I've been lucky enough to sample on my travels. I'm happy to say I haven't met a chocolate that I don't like.

Don't rush the immersion blending for this recipe, it really does the trick in changing this from liquid with powder particles in it, to a rich emulsified white chocolate bar that's off-the-charts good.

1. Prepare a baking sheet with parchment paper or set silicone moulds on a baking sheet.
2. Whisk the cream powder, allulose, lecithin, and salt together. Set aside.
3. Melt the cacao butter very slowly in a double boiler or a bowl atop a saucepan full of water. Add the coconut oil as the butter is melting.
4. Remove the bowl from the saucepan. Stir in the dry mixture and the vanilla. Use an immersion blender to emulsify and smooth out the chocolate. Blend well. The mixture will seem to thicken at first; keep mixing and it will loosen again.
5. Pour the liquid chocolate in a prepared tray or silicone moulds. Refrigerate for about 15 to 30 minutes, or until solid.

❖ **VARIATION: WHITE CHOCOLATE BARK**

Add 4 to 6 ounces chopped mixed nuts and dried fruit. Try the dehydrated cranberries from Blissfully Cran-Bars (page 205). Some fruit and nuts have higher carbs than others.

Pantry Items

A pantry switchover occurs when you start a healthy lifestyle. Slowly increase specialty items instead of doing an entire or fast switch.

The food items in the following list are not requirements for healthy cooking; these are considered extras. Most of your diet should be focused on whole unprocessed foods such as those grown by a farmer. The easiest path to health can be found around the perimeter of a store in the produce, meat, and fish sections.

Many of the items below are available in the natural or health food sections of supermarkets or can be purchased online. No matter where you live, choose the cleanest ingredients available to you: generally speaking, the longer the ingredients list, the more additives and preservatives lurk inside. Do the best you can with what you have. Add your own flavour components and stay away from processed foods as much as possible. Read the ingredients label on each product to determine what best suits your own health needs.

Allulose. A naturally occurring zero glycemic sugar that tastes about 70 per cent as sweet as sugar. Recommended for use in sauces, ice creams, and puddings but not in cakes and cookies. In baked goods, allulose has a gelling effect and cakes and cookies will not rise the way you want.

Brown sweetener. A brown sugar replacement. Clean versions are difficult to find but they exist. For most recipes, it is safe to switch out to regular powdered sweetener without detriment to the taste.

Buffalo mozzarella cheese. A round specialty buffalo cheese usually made from buffalo milk, most often suspended in a liquid. Find it with the specialty cheeses.

Butter. We recommend salted butter. Salt is a flavour enhancer that works equally well in sweets as it does in savoury foods. We used salted butter to test all our recipes.

Celeriac or celery root. A versatile faux-tato with a bland taste that is similar to that of a potato. It is suitable for roasting and for use in soups, stews, and purées. It looks like a turnip root with an unruly hairdo. Find it in the produce aisle.

Ceylon cinnamon. A mild, high-quality spice known as true cinnamon. Most cinnamon sold in supermarkets is the cheaper cassia cinnamon; cassia is high in coumarin, which can cause liver damage. Ceylon cinnamon can be found in most health food stores.

Chanterelle. A foraged mushroom, it may be substituted for any mushroom. Farmers markets are the best places to find these.

Chayote squash. A low glycemic fruit that is a part of the gourd family. It looks like a cross between a Granny Smith apple and an odd-shaped pear and is similar to apple in texture but without the sweetness. Use gloves when peeling this fruit. Find this in larger grocery stores with the other squash or in food specialty stores.

Chili garlic sauce. A starch-free sriracha replacement. Look for it in the international aisle of the supermarket.

Coconut sauce. A fermented coconut sauce product. This soy sauce replacement enhances flavour, but it may be omitted in most recipes. Find it in the health food section of bigger grocery stores, select health food stores, and bulk stores. This is not coconut milk.

Cream of tartar + baking soda. A replacement for baking powder, which is usually high in starch. For every 1 teaspoon baking powder, substitute 1/2 teaspoon cream of tartar plus 1/4 teaspoon baking soda.

Egg white powder. Protein powder derived from egg whites stabilizes baked goods and can be blended into shakes and used in place of whey. Whey is a bulking agent that can impede weight loss. Available online and in health food stores.

Fish sauce. A Worcestershire sauce (usually contains gluten and other additives) replacement and flavour enhancer. It may be omitted in most recipes. Find it in the international section of larger supermarkets and some health food stores. This product contains a minimal amount of sugar, which is mostly used up in fermentation.

Flax meal. Ground flax, or flax seed ground or powdered at home. Find it in the health food section of larger supermarkets, bulk stores, and some health food stores.

Food-grade oil. Essential oils that are food grade are GRAS (generally recognized as safe by the Canadian Food Inspection Agency). Purchase these at any store that sells craft and quality baking supplies.

Oils. Avoid inflammatory vegetable oils. Use lard, bacon fat, tallow (beef fat), olive oil, avocado oil, coconut oil, or other cold-pressed oils. Choose unflavoured and liquid coconut oils for most recipes that list coconut oil as an ingredient. Use these oils to grease baking pans.

Halloumi. A specialty cheese that can be grilled, fried, or deep-fried. Find this with the high-end cheeses at grocery stores.

Hearts of palm. A vegetable harvested from the inner core and growing bud of certain palm trees; use as a pasta replacement. Available with the canned vegetables at grocery stores.

Heavy whipping cream powder. A shelf-stable, dehydrated heavy cream powder that can be added to baked goods. This can be purchased online or in health food stores.

Keto products. Treat commercially available keto bread, crackers, bars, and all such products as suspect. Most of these products are no healthier than non-"keto" food. Avoid sugar, starches, grains, additives, and gluten. Check all the ingredients carefully.

Konjac (noodles). Also known as shirataki. From the konjac root of South America. Find in the health food or international section of supermarkets and some health food stores. Ensure that these are not soy based. Soy is considered an inflammatory hormone interruptor that is particularly nasty for women.

Korean chili flakes. Often known as gochugaru, this chili has a mild to moderate spicy taste with a hint of sweetness. The vibrant glossy red flakes appear almost crystallized. It is traditionally made from sun-dried seedless Korean hot red peppers. Available online, in international sections in supermarkets, and in Asian grocery stores.

Monk fruit. A sweetener, also known as lo han guo or Swingle fruit, from a small round fruit native to southern China. Available in bulk stores, health food stores, and online.

Nutritional yeast. Deactivated yeast with a cheesy flavour that is sold as a food product. These yellow flakes, granules, or powder are found in the health food section of supermarkets, in bulk stores, and in health food stores. A great source of vitamin B.

Psyllium husk. Find this in the natural food section of supermarkets, bulk stores, and some health food stores. Do not use psyllium husk from the pharmacy section—it will likely be flavoured and full of additives.

Pork rinds. Dehydrated and then puffed (by deep-frying) pig skin. These should be pale beige; if they are darker or flavoured/coloured, they are covered in a spice blend or flavourings which likely contain MSG.

Protein shakes. Many protein shakes have a whey base, which is a bulking agent that can cause a blood glucose spike. It is not conducive to weight control. We recommend making shakes using egg white powder.

Salt. We recommend a good-quality Himalayan pink or sea salt. Most table salts use sugar (check box ingredients) as a preservative and stabilizer.

Shirataki (noodles). See konjac (noodles).

Sour cream. Most sour creams contain starch. For anyone trying to reduce carbs and sugar, starches are the equivalent to a super sugar and should be avoided; they will spike blood glucose levels more than sugar does. Find starchless sour cream in larger supermarkets. Crème fraiche or plain unsweetened yogurt may be substituted for sour cream.

Sumac. A Middle Eastern spice that tastes mildly like bacon. Available in the international sections of supermarkets and online.

Sunflower lecithin. An emulsifier that helps to stabilize mixtures and prevent separating. Lecithin is a fatty substance naturally found in the human body and foods such as eggs and sunflower seeds. It is an alternative to soy lecithin.

White balsamic vinegar. This vinegar tastes like regular balsamic vinegar, but it has less sugar. Find with the vinegars in supermarkets.

Xanthan gum. A thickening agent for soups, stews, and gravies. Find in the health food section of supermarkets and some health food stores.

Index

A

Addie's (Billy Miner) Cream Pie 200
Addie's cream (coffee-flavoured) ice cream 239
Apple Coffee Cake 234
Avo BLT Chaffle 38
Avocado and Tomato Salad 93

B

Bacon Mayonnaise 272
bacon mix 26
Baked Cinnamon French Toast 41
Baked Garlic Breadsticks 14
Baker's Magic (Pan) Release 273
Banana Cream Pie 202
BBQ in a Bowl 88
béchamel sauce 98
beef dishes 18, 85, 154, 156, 164, 179, 187, 192, 197, 277
Bell Pepper Egg Rings 43
Best Faux-Tato Salad 95
Blackberry Grill Sauce 273
Blackened Salmon 132
Blissfully Cran-Bars 205
Blizzards 207
Blondies 209
Blue Cheese Ball 274
Blueberry Cream Cake 210
Blueberry Pancakes 44
Boston Cream Poke Cake 212
Braised Baby Bok Choy 96
Braised Beef Ribs and Daikon 154
bread 14, 288
brown butter sauce 116
Brownies 209
butter pecan ice cream 239
buttercream icing 249

C

Caesar dressing 137
candied ginger 269
caramel sauce 225
Carrot Top Chimichurri 120
cauliflower 111, 127, 128
Celeriac, Leek, and Bacon Soup 63

champagne reduction 30
Cheese Ball 274
cheesecake 222, 225, 253
Cheesy Beef Bake 156
cherry chocolate ice cream 239
cherry gastrique 190
Chicken à la King 159
Chicken and Ginger Noodle Bowl 64
chicken dishes 16, 24, 60, 64, 68, 70, 77, 85, 159, 161, 164, 169, 174, 180
Chicken Lombardy 161
Chicken Nuggets 16
chicken scratchins 70
chocolate carrot loaf 269
Chocolate Chip Cookie Skillet 217
chocolate drizzle 200
chocolate fudge ice cream 239
Chocolate Faux Guinness Cake 218
chocolate sauce 218
Cinco de Mayo BBQ Sauce 171
Cinnamon Coffee Cake Loaf 220
Cocktail Sauce 274
cod dishes 134, 142, 151
Cod in Tarragon Butter 134
coffee ice cream 239
cranberry compote 222
cranberries, dried 205
Cranberry Cheesecake 222
Cranberry Meatballs 18
Cranberry Orange Biscotti 205
Cream of Chicken Soup 68
Creamy Carbonara Primavera with Bacon 163
Crispy Caesar Salmon 137
Crustless Salted Caramel Cheesecake 225
Curry Shrimp 148

D

Dark Chocolate Tart with Raspberry Coulis 227
Devilled Egg Unwich 23
dill aioli 24
Dill-Lightful Wings 24
Donair Meat and Sweet Sauce 276
Double Chocolate Peanut Butter Bars 230
duck 190

E

Egg Roll in a Bowl 164
Eggnog 278
Eggplant Lasagna with Béchamel 98
egg dishes 23, 38, 43, 46, 50, 53, 56, 58
English toffee sauce 279

F

Faux Apple Cake 232
Faux Mac and Cheese 103
Faux Tater Tots 104
faux-tatoes 95, 104, 125
fennel (roasted) 111
Fennel Slaw 106
Fennel Soup 73
Figgy(less) Pudding 279
Fish Cakes Eggs Benny 46
fish dishes 79, 131-151
Fish Stick Tacos 139
five-spice mix 32
French toast 41
French Vanilla Ice Cream 237

G

ganache 212, 229, 253
Ginger Crème Brûlée 240
granola bars 286
Greek Omelette 50
Grilled Spatchcock Chicken 169

H

Ham, Mushroom, and Tomato Hash 53
Hard Tortilla Shells 139
hash 53
herbed spinach tots 104
Hickory Sticks 26
hoisin-style sauce 66
hollandaise sauce 48
Honey Mustard Glaze 281
Honey-ish Balsamic Pork Chops 173

I

Ice creams 237-239
Irish Colcannon 108

Irish Whiskey Frosting 218
Irish Whiskey Sauce 184
Italian Wedding Soup 74

J

Jakey Buns (Tea Biscuits) 283
Jalapeño Popper Soup 77
Jamaican Rum Cake 242
Jerk Meatballs 18

L

lamb dishes 29, 192
Lamb Kofta 27
Leeks (roasted) 111
Lemon and Dill Baked Cod 142
lemon-butter mix 142
Lemon Chicken 174
lemon vinaigrette 106
Lilac Love Cake 244
lilac syrup 244
Lime Chiffon Cake with Praline Crumb 249
Lisa and Brett's Nanaimo Cheesecake 253
lobster devilled eggs 23

M

maple garlic sauce 171
Maple Syrup Substitute 283
maple pecan ice cream 239
Margherita Pizza 287
Marsala cream chicken 161
Marshmallow 284
Masala-Spiced Pork Chops 177
Mayonnaise 272
meatballs 18, 197
Meatballs in Red Sauce 197
meatloaf 18
minty rum syrup 251
Mixed Berry Crumble Squares 254
Mongolian Beef 179
Mushroom Pie 54
Mushroom Ragout, 183
Mustard Vinaigrette 285

N

no-bake ganache filling 228
noodle bowl 64

O

OMJ Half-Baked Chicken, 180
orange chocolate ice cream 239
orange spice pork belly 31
Oven Roasted Veg 111

P

Pan-Seared Scallops 30
pastry cream 253
pancakes 44
Peanut Butter Granola 286
Peony and Pistachio Cake 256
Piccata Style Trout with Capers 144
pickling brine 24
pie crust 54
pie (savoury) 54, 56
pie (sweet) 200, 202, 227
piperade vinaigrette 115
pizza 287
pomegranate jam 27
pork belly 32
pork chops 173, 177, 183, 184
Pork Chops with Irish Whiskey Sauce 184
Pork Chops with Mushroom Ragout 183
pork dishes 18, 32, 74, 85, 164, 173, 177, 183, 184, 189, 192, 194
Portuguese Fish Stew 79
Protein Pizza Crust 289
pumpkin pancakes 44

Q

Quiche Lorraine 56

R

ranch mix 26
raspberry coulis 227
Ratatouille 113
Ravioli with Brown Butter Sauce 116
Red Pepper Meatloaf 187
red sauce 196
Roasted Carrots with Carrot Top Chimichurri 120
Roasted Green Tomato Soup 80
Roasted-Garlic-and-Parm-Crusted Pork 189
roasted garlic butter 14
roasted tomato sauce 98
Roly Poly 259
rum and butter syrup 242

S

S'piked Lilac Lemonade 246
salads 93-95, 106
salmon 132, 137, 146
Salmon en Papillote 146
Salsa Egg Skillet 58
salsa (fish) 141
scallops 30
Seared Duck Breast with Cherry Gastrique 190
Shepherd's Pie 192
Shortbread Cookies 260
shrimp 148

Skeddi Ohs 122
slaw 139
Slow-Roasted Maple Pork Loin 194
soft tortilla wraps 141
soups 61-89
sour cream and onion mix 26
Sour Cream Glazed Donuts 262
Soured Dough Bread 290
Soused Shrimp 148
spice mixes 26
Spicy Baconnaise 272
Spinach Dip 292
sticky lilacs 244
sticky Phoenix sauce 32
stinging nettle pesto 83
Stinging Nettle Soup 83
Strawberry and Cream Mini Muffins 265
Strawberry Shortcake Deconstructed 267
strawberry spinach salad 93
streusel topping 210
Stuffed Polpette al Sugo 197
sugo 196
Sunday Roast Confit Faux-Tatoes 125
sweet 'n' sour sauce 16

T

Taco Pie 156
Taco Soup 85
Tangy Sweet 'n' Sour Sauce 16
tarragon butter 134
Tartar Sauce 293
Tea Biscuits 283
Teriyaki Sauce 293
tomato jam 151
tortillas 131, 139
triple-chocolate brownies 209
trout 144
Turmeric-Crusted Cod with Tomato Jam 151

V

Veggie Curry—Nine Gem Korma 127

W

Walnut Ginger Carrot Cake 269
Warm Bacon Dip 35
Wedge Fries 125
White Asparagus (Spargel) Soup 86
White Chocolate 295
white chocolate bark 295
White Chocolate Mousse 222
Whole Roasted Cauliflower 128
wings 24

Acknowledgements

Thanks to everyone on the Boulder team who helped me so much: to Gavin and Amanda Will for trusting my vision; to Stephanie Porter, the ever-patient editor who turned my own inner ramblings to a polished and presentable piece of culinary art; to Iona Bulgin for the impeccable scrutinous eye; and to Tanya Montini for the incredible layout and design and cover.

To Maria for forging the path and being a fabulous mentor.

To Janet for being one of my biggest fans and also my friend. For trusting my capabilities and giving me a forum to reach our community with my food as well as my art. You are appreciated more than you know.

To Roary for including us and for fuelling my desire to play in the commercial kitchen in a way I never thought possible. Thank you for mentoring, providing valuable insight, and always being my go-to for answers to my questions. I'm looking forward to many more wonderful culinary adventures together.

To G for being my recipe tester, my sounding board, and my best freind. When we became a we, I had no idea how close we would become, how much we would grow and conquer together, how many puppies we would love. Thank you for putting up with my wild shenanigans with a smile, a hand held out, and a "Come on we goes!" attitude. Thank you for encouraging me to be all I can be and for adoring the baby goat that I am. And for being okay that the answer to the question "Who's lame-brained idea was this anyways!?" is always me. You are the other half of my heart. You are the one. I choose you.

To Addie, my most honest advisor and my rock. Every hair on your head is adored and there is no greater or pure love than the one I feel for you.

To Kayla, my very own white-hatted Olivia Pope. You have become one of my most trusted advisors and I am so grateful for your presence in my life. Thank you for always having my back, helping to "spin" my words into magic, and always coming to my aid. You are the daughter I never had and you mean the world to me.

To Nan and Mom (posthumously) for starting me on a journey of love in the kitchen. The times I spent by both your sides watching, stirring, and sampling fed my heart as well as my inquisitive mind.

To Isadora, Calliope, and Squishi for being faithful watchers of *The Mommy and Daddy Cooking Show*.

Many people ask me where I get my recipes. You can see my secret in this photograph. That's my grandmother's handwriting. I believe she was absolutely brilliant to use up the white space in her cookbooks with notes The notes she made in her cookbooks are precious. We hope you use the white space in this and all of our cookbooks to pen your own loving touches.